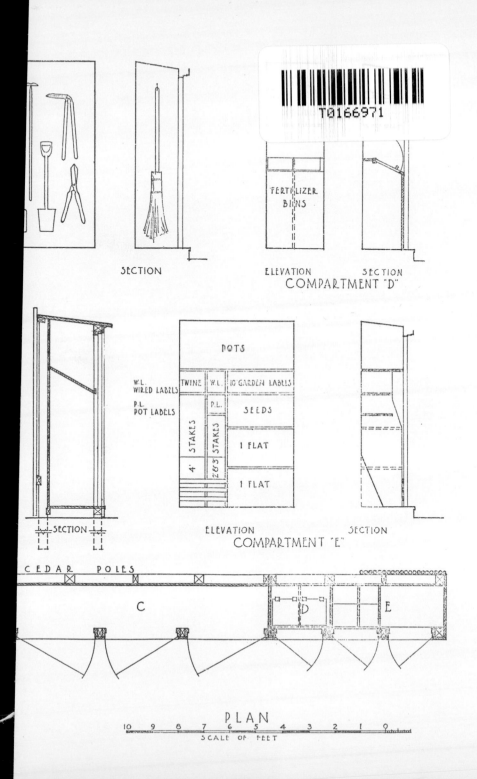

SECTION

ELEVATION   SECTION

FERTILIZER BINS

COMPARTMENT "D"

POTS

W.L. WIRED LABELS	TWINE	W.L.	10 GARDEN LABELS
P.L. POT LABELS		P.L.	SEEDS
	4' STAKES	2&6'3' STAKES	1 FLAT
			1 FLAT

SECTION

ELEVATION   SECTION

COMPARTMENT "E"

CEDAR POLES

C   D   E

PLAN

10 9 8 7 6 5 4 3 2 1 0

SCALE OF FEET

DESIGN IN THE LITTLE GARDEN

DESIGN IN THE LITTLE GARDEN

Fletcher Steele

Introduction by Robin Karson

LIBRARY OF AMERICAN LANDSCAPE HISTORY

AMHERST

LC 2011015000
ISBN 978-1-55849-907-2

Designed by Jonathan D. Lippincott
Set in Scotch Roman
Printed and bound by KHL Printing Co. Pte Ltd

Library of Congress Cataloging-in-Publication Data

Steele, Fletcher.
  Design in the little garden / Fletcher Steele ; introduction by
Robin Karson.
    p. cm.
  "The text of Design in the Little Garden is reprinted from the
original edition published by Atlantic Monthly Press (Boston, 1924)."
  ISBN 978-1-55849-907-2 (cloth : alk. paper) 1. Gardens—Design.
2. Landscape gardening. I. Library of American Landscape History. II. Title.
  SB472.45.S74 2011
  712—dc22

                                                        2011015000

British Library Cataloguing in Publication data are available.

Frontispiece: Fletcher Steele at Naumkeag, c. 1930.
Courtesy The Trustees of Reservations.

Historical plans and photographs credited to SUNY ESF Archives are
from the Fletcher Steele Manuscript Collection, Terence J. Hoverter College
Archives, F. Franklin Moon Library, State University of New York College of
Environmental Science and Forestry, Syracuse, N.Y.

CONTENTS

Preface   ix

Introduction by Robin Karson   xiii

DESIGN IN THE LITTLE GARDEN
by Fletcher Steele

FOR NANCY

PREFACE

Among the thousands of books published about garden design, there are very few that manage to get at so many vital aspects of the topic as pungently as Fletcher Steele's *Design in the Little Garden*. Like many of his gardens, Steele's book is both charming and fit—goals that can be maddeningly elusive, as any gardener knows. The decision to reprint Steele's book, one of only two he wrote, would seem obvious, given his current stature as one of America's most important landscape architects. But uncovering, and then recovering, Steele's reputation has been a long process.

When I began working on Steele's biography in the early 1980s, few people were aware of his work, and many of those who did know of it harbored a sense of Steele as an outsider. The homophobic culture at the Harvard School of Graduate Design dominating the years after World War II is in some measure responsible for the erasure. My research was encouraged by individuals who had either known Steele, worked for him, or viewed him as a source of inspiration for their own work. Among the first group were Vincent Merrill and several clients; among the second were Peter Hornbeck, Harry Hoover, and Arthur Sylvester. The third included Garret Eckbo and, most vociferously, Dan Kiley.

On more than one occasion, Kiley expressed the opinion that Steele was "the only good designer" working during the first half of the century, a statement that was no doubt an exaggeration, especially given Kiley's admiration for Warren H. Manning, who had been his boss as well as Steele's. I see now that, beyond Steele's experimental nature, elegant designs, and rich use of history, Kiley may also have felt a camaraderie with Steele stemming from his own frustrations with Harvard, where Beaux-Arts notions of control enflamed the famous triad of mavericks which also included James Rose and Garrett Eckbo.

That said, Steele benefited enormously from his Beaux-Arts education, and he also benefited greatly from his study with Warren Manning, who invested his young associate with a thorough grounding in Olmstedian principles, particularly a high regard for the genius loci. These two sets of ideas provided a sure footing for Steele as he explored a third wellspring of inspiration: the hopes, dreams, personalities, and preferences of his clients. It is perhaps this aspect of *Design in the Little Garden* that outshines every other—Steele's sense that the best gardens reflect the idiosyncrasies of those living in them.

The new Library of American Landscape History reprint of *Design in the Little Garden* is dedicated to Nancy R. Turner, founding president of the Library of American Landscape History. Nancy, with her late husband, Richard L. Turner, commissioned one of Steele's last and finest gardens, in Pittsford, New York, and she knew Steele well. She came to know of my work in American landscape history over the course of my research on the Steele biography, offering help at every turn. When I approached her with the idea of founding an organization dedicated to publishing books in the field of landscape studies, she very gamely agreed and together we launched LALH. *Design in the Little Garden* is the twenty-fifth volume published by the organization. The gratitude and affection I have felt for Nancy Turner throughout this venture defy my powers of expression. Some thoughts lie too deep for words.

•

This edition of *Design in the Little Garden* has been made possible by generous gifts from charitable funds advised by Nancy Turner's four children, Richard Turner, Sarah Turner, James Turner, and Molly Turner: Westchester Community Foundation–Esplanade Fund, California Community Foundation–Aurora-Viburnum Fund, Calvert Foundation–Blackhaw Fund, and Calvert Foundation–Arrowwood Fund. I thank these organizations and all the members of the Turner family for their encouragement and generosity.

I also thank Carol Betsch and Mary Bellino for their fine editorial suggestions on the introduction and Jonathan Lippincott for his elegant design. As always, I am grateful to the staff and to the Trustees of the Library of American Landscape History for their staunch support of our program and mission.

The reprint edition is a facsimile of the first edition except that the gatefold originally inserted between pages 80 and 81 is here reproduced on the endpapers.

INTRODUCTION TO THE REPRINT EDITION
Robin Karson

Fletcher Steele (1885–1971) designed and wrote during a time of tumultuous change in his profession. *Design in the Little Garden,* published in 1924 as part of the Little Garden Series, captures the sense of possibility that Steele and his landscape architectural colleagues felt as the nation's population swelled and the middle class spilled out of the cities into new suburbs. Little Garden Series editor Louisa Yeomans King and legions of other reform-minded authors, including Steele, felt it their duty to take on the seemingly monumental task of educating these homeowners in matters of taste.

Steele was an able soldier in the crusade. One of the best-known landscape designers of the early twentieth century, he also opined with the most engaging voice, his sharp wit tempered by affectionate exasperation. "Petunias and nasturtiums are grown on gaunt native ledges," he complains in *Design in the Little Garden.* "Begonias edge beds of absurdly clumped ever-greens. Salvia is everywhere. Little houses are belted with bulging shrubs as mud rolls out from under a footfall."

The problems Steele tackles in this diminutive book transcend horticulture, however. He also addresses architectural and planning issues, recommending several innovative strategies for suburban house design. These include putting the kitchen at the front of the house (so that the living room can overlook a rear garden) and siting the garage near the street to lessen the area sacrificed to a driveway. Steele also criticizes zoning laws that require freestanding garages and setback requirements that center houses on narrow lots, creating useless, dark corridors on either side.

Presciently, Steele's book emphasizes cohesion and utility. "The good plan considers the whole lot as the unit into which each detail must fit as may be best—not only for itself but for every other detail on the place. There should not be one square foot of wasted area on a lot any more than there would be in a house that is well planned." In the course of guiding an imaginary couple through the exercise of buying a new home, Steele gives life to these principles, prophesying the age of functionalism four years before Clarence Stein and Henry Wright implemented similar strategies in the planned town of Radburn, N.J.[1]

Steele organized his book for clarity and ease of use; brief chapters focus on both process ("Buying Land") and features ("The Flower Garden," "Toolhouse, Cold Frames," "Garden-Furnishing," etc.). The landscape architect's advice on how to build steps is typical in its down-to-earth tone. "Where stone is cheap, stone steps are easy to build, either with or without mortar. Except in much 'slicked up' places it is prettier to lay them dry, so that plants will grow between them. What matter if they get heaved a bit during the winter? An hour in the spring with a crow-bar and shovel will set them sufficiently to rights." It should be said that the sometimes imperious Steele did not often use a crowbar himself. Indeed, he claimed that he did all his grading with a cane, and when asked how that was possible, replied, "You point at a pile of dirt, and tell your workman move that"—he redirected his cane—"over there. It works every time."[2]

Steele spent his childhood on a farmstead in Pittsford, New York, near the Erie Canal, his early world populated with horse-drawn carriages, streetcars, and trains, the preferred method of transportation to nearby Rochester, which was even then becoming a sophisticated city. The Steeles grew a mix of vegetables and flowers in old-fashioned beds laid out according to common sense. The future designer wholly approved of the fitness of this garden, a principle he promoted throughout *Design in the Little Garden* and one that would guide his own work, too.

He got his start in 1908 working for Warren H. Manning—having been lured away from his graduate studies at Harvard with the promise of an unpaid job. After six years in the office (he eventually did receive a salary) and with Manning's blessing, he left the senior practitioner's firm to set up his own Boston-based practice. First, he treated himself to a grand tour of English and European gardens, parks, and cities that reinforced his Harvard-bred, Beaux-Arts-influenced sense of landscape architecture as a fine art. Steele would later draw parallels between his own garden-making and painting and sculpture, citing influences as disparate as Brancusi (in his design for the South Lawn of Naumkeag, in Stockbridge, Massachusetts), and Titian (in a remarkable spiraling layout for the Robert and Helen Stoddard garden, in Worcester, Massachusetts).

On his first trip abroad, Steele discovered classical French parks, squares, and gardens, which immediately became a source of exhilaration and inspiration. "The Place Vendôme in Paris is perfect," he wrote in his travel notes. "It is the simplest of all in design and execution; its proportions are the most majestic; its decoration superb. If it possesses some of the superhuman coldness of perfection which threatens Raphael and chills the Venus de Medici, it is in the company where each of us would wish our work to be."[3]

Steele's own work, while often reflective of French ideas, was, in fact, the opposite of cold. Emotionally charged, playful, and richly laced with quotations from gardens around the globe, his designs also reverberated with the genius loci, a force that had shaped the work of Warren Manning as it had Manning's mentors, Frederick Law Olmsted and Charles Eliot. Although Steele continued to rely on the Beaux-Arts methods he had absorbed at

Harvard, he soon began to see the garden in more imaginative terms—as he put it, a setting for his clients' dreams. "Dreaming enables us to withdraw into ourselves for brief moments and rests us," he told one audience. "It is good and if the garden makes it easier and pleasant to dream, then it is a good garden."[4] Eventually there were more than five hundred such designs.[5]

Among Steele's first and most important clients was Charlotte Whitney Allen, whose tiny backyard in Rochester provided him with commissions for five decades. He told one magazine editor that he considered it in many ways his finest garden, despite its size.[6] Allen may have been unique in her request for

Charlotte Whitney Allen garden, view from house terrace. (Photograph by Felice Frankel, 1987)

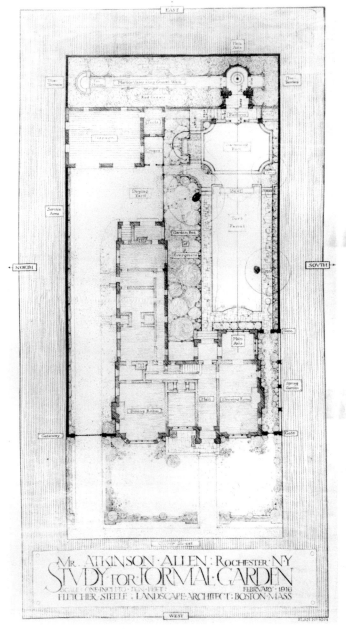

Allen garden plan, 1916. (SUNY ESF College Archives)

no flowers—in 1914 the Arts and Crafts borders promulgated by Gertrude Jekyll and her English colleagues were still much in demand. (Mrs. Whitney was not kidding about the flowers. One day neighbors spotted her on a ladder, cutting lavender blossoms off the wisteria that covered one side of the house and cursing Steele, who had promised her that it would never bloom.) The repose of this strongly composed, tailored space may have been an inspiration for Steele's chapter on the green garden—"a cool quiet green place, rarely drawing attention to itself, but content to be, like a dim, old room full of books—a place to live and think, and perhaps at times to dream."

An equally important work, Naumkeag, begun in 1926, was laid out over many years as a series of vistas and panoramic views as well as circumscribed gardens. Here, too, one sees many prin-

Naumkeag, Afternoon Garden plan, bird's-eye view, 1930. (SUNY ESF College Archives)

Naumkeag, Afternoon Garden. (*Photograph by Carol Betsch, 2002*)

ciples at work that were first articulated in *Design in the Little Garden*. Steele's initial design was for the Afternoon Garden, a feature inspired by an outdoor room Mabel Choate had visited on a recent Garden Club of America trip to California. Nothing so comfortable was to be found in the stiff c. 1885 layout Nathan Barrett had designed for her parents, which Choate was about to inherit. Steele sited the new "room" at the south end of the Stanford White cottage—where it would not impinge on Barrett's fine Victorian design—delineating transparent walls with oak columns and making a carpet of pink gravel and lobelia and, after the lobelia began to sulk, black coal.

   In the center he created a shallow pool whose glass bottom he painted black. "Sky, flowers, foliage, light and shadow seem more brilliant when reflected from a black quiet pool than when seen directly," he observes in his chapter on garden furnishing. Four scalloped fountain basins surround the pool; the pretty marble shells were based on originals at the Generalife. Fountains, Steele warns, are often "depressing, even ugly, when without the spouting water that is necessary to complete their design. . . . Consequently, it is worthwhile getting fountains—especially on small places where they are always conspicuous—which look well as decoration when the water does not play."

Although Mabel Choate did not share Charlotte Allen's antipathy toward flowers, Steele used bloom sparingly at Naumkeag. It makes a sequential appearance in the c. 1937 Chinese Temple Garden, a walled garden carpeted with moss and bare

Naumkeag, Chinese Temple Garden. (Photograph by Carol Betsch, 2002)

earth. Tree peonies erupt in pastel tones each May; a Father Hugo rose showers cascades of golden petals in June; brilliant red pelargonium fill royal blue pots for the remainder of summer. "Too many flower-gardens become slave drivers," Steele notes in his book. "Their owners never dare sit down in them. Weeds spring up while the back is straightening. Faded flowers forever call for the scissors. Late or diseased larkspur or phlox must be doctored, coddled, and worried over. At its best, they have a dangerous tendency to resemble the White Queen's condiment in *Through the Looking Glass*, 'Jam to-morrow and jam yesterday—but never jam to-day.'"

When circumstances (or opportunity) called for it, Steele's work could be intensely floriferous. His design for Catherine and John Bullard, in Dartmouth, Massachusetts, beginning in 1948, featured an orange, yellow, and deep red primrose garden inspired, he later claimed, by a Persian carpet. In a 1936 garden in Gloucester, Massachusetts, Steele drew attention away from

Bullard primrose garden, spring. *(Photograph by Fletcher Steele. SUNY ESF College Archives)*

Ornamental border, Gloucester, Mass. (Photograph by Fletcher Steele. SUNY ESF College Archives)

a competing ocean view, which also included unappealing house backs, using an unexpected combination of red begonias, yellow canna lilies, and blue-toned grasses to eye-popping effect. "Painters realize better than gardeners that, given a sufficient volume, all flower colors may be mingled with impunity," he writes in his chapter on flower gardens.

Provocatively, Steele's book defends the despised Victorian convention known as carpet-bedding. "Wholesale condemnation is a dangerous thing, especially in matters of taste. Because carpet-bedding was bad, the world jumped to the conclusion that all planting done with regular patterns must necessarily be ugly and stiff. It took a long time for people to realize that under certain circumstances nothing but this type of design was appropriate, especially in formal gardens which had any flavor of the French style." He continues, "As time goes on I believe that the development of honesty among gardeners—which means always a growth of individual taste—will reveal the fact that many people are really fond of this classic sort of garden design, just as many people are fond of classic austerity and fine proportion in houses, even where it can be gotten only at the expense of coziness."

Steele's last major garden, designed for Richard and Nancy Turner, in the landscape architect's hometown of Pittsford, marked one final return to French formality, tempered by a loose American style of planting. The methods he used in the c. 1963 layout were presaged by several ideas he first articulated in *Design in the Little Garden:* "Nature has a way of mixing things up. She is more apt to line up a tree, two tall bushes, a clump of fern, a rock, another tree. . . . Take a leaf out of such a planting-book in composing the lawn borders. Remember, too, that Nature's best effects are always a phase in the war for the survival of the fittest. Overplant everywhere, mixing up varieties of many things, with a preponderance of two or at most three varieties from among the many used."

Richard and Nancy Turner garden, North Vista, spring. (Photograph by Felice Frankel, 1987)

The trees and shrubs in the garden's North Vista formed a tapestry of seasonally modulating color and texture. The extensive and varied plant list mixed red maple with flowering quince, ginkgo, four types of spruce, Japanese pagoda tree, witch hazel, holly, and a range of other species of shrubs and trees. At the end of his life, Steele had arrived at a true late style, the principles of his art, succinctly defined in his 1924 book, having been internalized to the point of spontaneous mastery.

In the final chapters of *Design in the Little Garden* Steele explores the quiet charm of long-established, smaller gardens in Italy, France, and England. He conjures up an Italian garden with a word painting that includes a shelter of grapevines, oil jars, a fig tree, an oleander, and strings of peppers hung under the eaves to dry. "Work and play both have their place. Use and ornament combine, then separate again, both present everywhere." Steele muses, "An efficiency expert could learn much from the extraordinarily practical and intensive way in which the land is employed and cultivated. Its use is beautiful. Its beauty is used. Is that the cause of the perfume of romance that hangs over it all?"

He goes on to praise the immaculate and often microscopic French town garden, invariably enclosed with high walls and yet, as he points out, always in possession of a tree whose shade cooled house as well as garden. Grass was used only where a green carpet was desired. Here "beds of violets, English ivy, and ferns are preferred to failing spotted grass-turf." Steele writes, "Where [the owner] has the sun, a grapevine grows over his door and a great rosebush fills the quiet place with perfume and color. Old shrubs soften the corners. Moss gathers under the ivy on the walls. Somewhere he sees the gray-blue sky. The parish church near by has a chime of bells."

Finally, Steele turns to England, where, as elsewhere, "withdrawal from the outer world—seclusion—is the first and most important of garden qualities." Seeing in the English garden "the order of art in control of nature," he reflects: "This is perhaps the apotheosis of man's objective effort, the greatest contribution that England has made to the fine arts. Of course, not all English gardens, especially grandiose English gardens, are beautiful. But the old small home-gardens are all that one dreams a garden should be."

Throughout his long career, Steele continued to publish frequently in both popular and professional magazines, on topics that ranged from horticulture to conservation, civic improvement, modernism, and space composition. He returned full force to the subject of European gardens in his second book, *Gardens and People* (1964), but with less success than his impressionistic treatments in the earlier book. *Design in the Little Garden* remains Steele's most authoritative publication on the panoply of issues related to his subject. It still offers bountiful, even brilliant advice to those making gardens of any size.

NOTES

1. For more on Steele and planning, see George B. Tobey, *A History of Landscape Architecture: The Relation of People to Environment* (New York: American Elsevier, 1973), 198–99. See also Robin Karson, *Fletcher Steele, Landscape Architect: An Account of the Gardenmaker's Life, 1885–1971*, rev. ed. (Amherst: Library of American Landscape History, 2003), 63–64.

2. Vincent Merrill (Lincoln, Mass.), interview by Robin Karson, March 4, 1987; see also Karson, *Fletcher Steele, Landscape Architect*, 266.

3. Fletcher Steele, "Europe, 1913" (travel diary written for Warren Manning), 15. Fletcher Steele Manuscript Collection, F. Franklin Moon Library, State University of New York College of Environmental Science and Forestry, Syracuse, N.Y. On Steele's trip see Karson, *Fletcher Steele, Landscape Architect*, 12–15.

4. Steele, "Westport, Connecticut" (undated lecture manuscript), 1–2. Fletcher Steele Papers, Manuscript Division, Library of Congress, Washington, D.C.

5. Steele's client files listed more than seven hundred commissions; not all of these were realized, and some were for churches, libraries, or other civic projects. But the vast majority were private gardens.

6. Steele, letter to Betty Blossom (garden editor at *House & Garden*), July 21, 1953, Steele Papers, Library of Congress.

DESIGN IN THE LITTLE GARDEN

A small Rock-Garden, 40 by 20 feet, whose wall at the left hides an unsightly building. The path represents a stream-bed through which trickles water on the way from fountain to pool. The stratification of the rock is kept parallel everywhere. (See Chapter VII.)

THE LITTLE GARDEN SERIES

DESIGN IN THE LITTLE GARDEN

BY

FLETCHER STEELE

With Illustrations

THE ATLANTIC MONTHLY PRESS
BOSTON

EDITOR'S PREFACE

" IT is perhaps," says a writer in the London *Times,* reviewing an American work on landscape design — " It is perhaps in a land whose horizons are still unfinished, that there is room for such an art as is set forth here."

If our general horizons are unfinished, what shall be said of those individual ones that confront and bound the gaze of thousands upon thousands at a distance of a hundred feet or less? Most of us with little ground are as yet entirely ignorant of the special need for design, for plan, in little spaces. And this fact and the lack of any town-plan are the foremost reasons for the absolute ugliness of the average small town of, say, the Middle West. To use John Bunyan's sentence, " In a word, it is every whit dreadful, being utterly without Order." True, in the beginnings of such towns there was ample excuse for lack of plan; the labor and toil of those beginnings precluded the thought of finer things. To-day this excuse does not hold. A hundred avenues of education in design for the town itself, and for the suburban lot, are open to a public eager for more life in the open air and determined to learn how best to use the feet, rods, acres, which may be or are theirs. It is for that public that this book is written.

I quote here from a recent letter of Mr. Steele's. " I believe first and foremost in common sense and practical convenience and only in a secondary way — though not divorced from these in any sense — in the necessity of creating beauty. The two should go together; but more, the study of those things that are around us, whether flowers or factories, will reveal glorious realms of pleasure in the beautiful aspects of even the most familiar things — if we will only train ourselves to see."

Fletcher Steele is a Fellow of the American Society of Landscape Architects. After Williams College and two years at the Harvard School of Landscape Architecture, he was for several years assistant to Warren H. Manning. His work, a large and active practice since 1914, has carried him as far west as Wyoming and as far south as Virginia; and study abroad, as well as war service, gave him opportunity — of which he was quick to make use — for observation of foreign gardens. Mr.

EDITOR'S PREFACE

Steele lectures on his subject, and has often contributed to current journals.

In *Design in the Little Garden* the writer has set forth not only the principles but the practice of gardening as an art. Reasons are at hand for every statement. And what could be more stimulating to serious thought on design in the small place than the three highly interesting chapters about Maple Cove Avenue? Throughout the book, however, Mr. Steele has been at great pains not to intimate too definitely what planting should be done. The other books of this series are taken up so largely with planting-problems, that, rather than go into further detail here, it has been taken for granted that readers would get their planting-information from earlier books and those to come. But, with such practical discussions as those on " The Green Garden " and " Service Features, Arbors, and Fences," there need be few mistakes in making the small lot as beautiful as it can be made. A forward-looking part of the book is that devoted to " Rock, Wild, and Wall Gardens "; and in the last part of that whose title is " The Flower Garden " there is a breadth of view seldom found in books on gardening. Does not the last chapter of this book, with its unusual heading, " The Traveler Sees the Little Garden," actually convey the charm of gardens French, English, Italian, leaving us acutely sensible of our own shortcomings, of our own poverty in garden charm?

Design in the Little Garden is one more of those rungs of the tentative ladder to beauty in the small garden, on which it is hoped that many will set foot. It is a ladder of aspiration. That many may climb it, is the hope of all who have had to do with its building, for it lifts toward better things in the planning and planting of gardens; and this means of ascent is all in the interest of the happiest of recreations, a recreation well within the domain of the arts.

LOUISA YEOMANS KING.

CONTENTS

I	BUYING LAND	.	.	.	.	.	.	.	.	3
II	ECONOMY OF GROUND-USE	.	.	.	.	.	.	11
III	OUTDOOR LIVING-ROOMS	.	.	.	.	.	19
IV	LAWNS — GREEN GARDENS	.	.	.	.	.	25
V	THE FLOWER GARDEN	.	.	.	.	.	.	35
VI	CUT-FLOWER, VEGETABLE, AND FRUIT GARDEN	.	.	48
VII	ROCK, WILD, AND WALL GARDENS	.	.	.	.	54
VIII	GRADING, STEPS, WALKS	.	.	.	.	.	60
IX	GARDEN-FURNISHING	.	.	.	.	.	.	63
X	SERVICE-FEATURES, ARBORS, FENCES	.	.	.	71
XI	TOOLHOUSE, COLD FRAMES	.	.	.	.	.	78
XII	EXAMPLES	.	.	.	.	.	.	.	.	83
XIII	DETAILS OF No. 13 MAPLE COVE AVENUE	.	.	.	89
	Formal Garden							
XIV	DETAILS OF No. 11 MAPLE COVE AVENUE	.	.	.	98
	Informal Garden							
XV	DETAILS OF No. 15 MAPLE COVE AVENUE	.	.	.	109
	A Wasteful Plan							
XVI	THE TRAVELER SEES THE LITTLE GARDEN	.	.	.	115

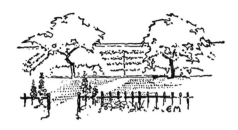

ILLUSTRATIONS

A Small Rock-Garden . . . . *Frontispiece*

House Well Screened behind Fence and Street Planting   6

A Small City Back-Yard 14

An Outdoor Living-Room 20

A Little Garden Next the House 44

A Shady Corner Terrace 60

A Black Mirror Pool in a Sunken Garden 66

A Summerhouse Connected with a Simple Arbor . . . 74

Details of a Small Toolhouse 80

Maple Cove Avenue 84

No. 13 Maple Cove Avenue 95

No. 11 Maple Cove Avenue 101

DESIGN IN THE LITTLE GARDEN

I

BUYING LAND

No one buys land on which to build without reasonable examination of the property. But most people do not go into the matter deeply enough. They are satisfied if sewer, water, electricity, and telephone are provided; if the neighbors are likable; if church and schools are at hand; if transportation by trolley or railroad is convenient; if the land presents no obstacle to economical building-operations.

The wise man goes further. He asks if the street is or is apt to become a through trunk-highway for trolleys, trucks, and motors. If so, shops and fruitstands will sooner or later push up around him like mushrooms. The street will become a source of incessant noise and dirt. As real estate it may increase in value for commercial purposes, while for a peaceful home site the true worth will rapidly deteriorate. Better far find some place on a side street with narrow driving-way and wide parking-space outside the sidewalk, a street laid out to be awkward to use rather than an easy short-cut for the peripatetical iceman and grocery-boy. This is especially desirable if at least some of the living-rooms are to face the street, as they will then be reasonably clean and quiet.

The future gardener will pay serious attention to soil conditions. A fair test can be made with a shovel. Here and there holes should be dug to the bottom of the loam to know its depth; more rarely, three feet deep to learn the character of the subsoil. For on it will depend much of the pains, expense, labor, and success of the future garden.

If rich deep loam is found, the way will be easy. The danger will lie in overcrowded plantations; slackening in the great battle against insects and plant diseases; or over-development of interest in the science of horticulture at the expense of arrangement and design. Either pride or indifference is then all too apt to overcome the gardener. He will never learn restraint. He will never know true humility or hope — the sweetest lessons of the garden. Only great ascetic souls, with the never satisfied ambitions of artists, should be given deep rich loam on which to begin their experience.

If one finds heavy clay, he will face a joyous struggle — joyous because crowned with certain success after a long fight. First, he must underdrain with farm tile to carry off the cold ground-water and let air into the overcrowded particles of soil. He must make foundations of broken stone, bricks, or gravel deep under his more particular plants. He must change the clay from intolerable stickiness when wet and rock-hard cakes when dry, to friable garden loam, by adding sand, ashes, manure, and humus; by trenching, ploughing, and liming to freeze and thaw, winter's soil compensation to the gardener. For a long time he must choose among plants only those which will endure stiff clay. But, as time goes on, he will be rewarded. His soil will become permanently rich and deep.

If, on the other hand, he finds nothing but sand or sandy gravel, his immediate undertaking will be less arduous, while the end will never come. Rain and snow drain quickly down through sand, taking with them the soluble virtues of the soil. Plant roots absorb food only in prepared soluble form. This is the reason for the use of the word, " available," so frequently seen in connection with commercial

fertilizers. Scientists tell us that all the elements necessary
to man or plant are to be found in rocks and sand. But
until they are prepared by chemical and physical reactions
they are as little available for the actual nourishment of
one as of the other. One of the profound satisfactions of
garden philosophy comes with the revelation that the life
process of plants turns useless material into food for
animals and men, while the corresponding life-process of
animals makes elements available for plants.

It is obvious that soluble plant-food is rapidly strained
away from sand that is constantly washed with rain and
snow-water. Even considerable particles of organic matter,
such as rotted plant-rootlets, wash down through loose grit
and disappear. Consequently it is necessary to compensate
for the steady loss of available plant food from above.
Year after year one must apply good loam, fertilizer, and
humus in quantity.

Humus is a general word with a specialized meaning for
gardeners. Humus is decaying or decayed organic matter,
which includes theoretically any sort of material that has
ever been part of a living thing, be it animal or plant. All
humus is food for plants, though more quickly available and
more concentrated in some forms than in others.

Modern civilization is more wasteful of organic matter —
for which there is an urgent need in our land — than of any
other one thing. Careless farmers exhaust their soils of
their humus-content. Cities waste their sewage. Mills pour
their wool-scouring water into the rivers. Individuals give
away garbage and burn their dried leaves. All is waste on
a hideously extravagant scale.

Farmers and gardeners must make up for the loss by
expensive fertilizers and commercial forms of humus, when

often their needs could be entirely supplied by what they throw away.

Soils are found in various combinations between pure sand and pure clay, all of them more or less constantly requiring different treatment, and all of them having an influence on the types of plant material which can be used successfully in the garden. To this extent they have a real influence on the design.

Sand and clay are important physical constituents of soils. Quite as important, though in part neglected until recently, are their chemical properties. Their influence on plant life has been shown to be largely through acidity or alkalinity. With great groups of plants these qualities are known to be all-important. Careful observations along these lines have only been begun. But it is known that many of the broad-leaved evergreens, such as rhododendron and mountain laurel, will not endure alkaline soils. The majority of important garden plants, however, seem to thrive in neutral or slightly alkaline soils. Soils can be made neutral or alkaline by the use of lime. It would appear from recent experiments that they can be made more acid with the use of aluminum sulphate. This discovery makes it possible to grow broad-leaved evergreens in all parts of this country, even where they have never before flourished, and has an important bearing on garden design, especially for winter and green gardens.

If the lot is bare of vegetation, one is free to start any sort of development. But the real results will be long in coming if shade is required. Trees take time to grow. Shade is a prime requisite of the livable garden. Without existing shade trees, a good plan will stress the importance of a large covered outdoor living-room.

House well screened behind fence and street planting, with garage built into the house and out of the way. This leaves room for a good-sized informal lawn and garden back of the house, and even the front porch is hidden and private.

One or two well-established trees on the open lot should receive serious consideration to the extent, in many cases, of actually controlling the location of all buildings and planting. Can the house be well located without badly damaging or cutting down the trees one wants to keep? Can the place be graded without burying existing growth under tons of soil? Whether or not large trees with their deep and sometimes gloomy shade should be near the house, where they act like heavy green window-shades that can never be drawn up, depends on individual taste. Experience goes to show that free circulation of air is desirable between trees and house, at least on three sides. Moreover, every room in the house should get a sun bath at least once during the daily passage of the garden god.

In respect to trees, one must foresee the immense side-spread of many varieties and the character of their shade, whether light, heavy, open, or thick like a blanket. In time the spindling stem planted thirty feet from the building may imperceptibly grow to be like the Old Man of the Sea on the back of the house.

When in the the garden area, trees are a great boon if their power is acknowledged and discounted while making the plan. Their shade is obnoxious to many flowering plants and shrubs. Their greedy roots are an incessant nuisance in garden beds. In some cases they appear to have a poisonous effect on certain plants which cannot endure their presence. The black walnut is an offender of this sort. Under most circumstances, the tree is more important to the gardener than the lesser plants, and the garden plan will be made accordingly.

Shady gardens — no matter how small the scale — have delightful qualities of mystery and comfort that are rarely equaled in sunny parterres where lawns and flowers flourish.

Then arises the question of topography. Flat land is easiest to manage conventionally by the gardener with no imagination. But charm and "atmosphere" are much sooner and more economically developed with the aid of slopes. The ideal small lot, perhaps, is one with the front on a level with or slightly higher than the street, sloping down toward the back. But, even when it runs downhill from the street, it can be managed if the house plan be made to fit the slope — not the other way round, as is ordinarily and wrongly done. A good deal of soil comes out of a cellar hole, which can be piled between house and street to bring the front yard high enough. Even if the slope toward the back is slight, any buildings beyond — being lower than the house — are less conspicuous. A slight difference of three or four feet is often a great advantage.

A lot sloping up from the street is probably better than a dead level. But it presents certain obstacles. The dirt from the cellar hole must be banked in behind terrace walls or carted away — an item of expense in either case. Drainage becomes an important problem, as both underground and surface water must be kept out of the house. Surface water can be easily carried around the building. Underground water is at times difficult to control. To be sure, this annoyance arises often on level land as well.

In any case, the foresighted gardener will prefer a sloping to a dead flat lot, if he has any imagination. Frankly, imagination is the only resource that can save economy from being drab, or at least pathetic. It can create a little paradise with the weeds of the field or the crumbs from the palace-garden table, out of a place that would remain stiff and ugly in spite of a score of gardeners without imagination. Fancy conceives a bit of planted wall, a step or two joining different levels, a path dipping down into a shady corner. On a natural slope such details are appropriately and cheaply constructed, while on flat land they are considerable matters to make, often running into thousands of dollars if well done.

There is, to be sure, a danger in willful, undisciplined imagination. It leads to discontent where lack of money or other circumstances prevent the achievement of preconceived ideas. The imagination that is helpful first makes a survey of available material and then says, " Here is my land — my tree — my house — my rose bush — my garbage. Let us set about making the best of them."

Aspect and prospect must be carefully studied, not only as they exist but as they may become. Will the open meadow all about soon be covered with houses? Will tall apartment buildings creep in? Is the neighborhood safe against the insinuation of ugly factories? On steep hills, many a small lot has an open view, assured for all time, which should be used to the utmost. Elsewhere, even a charming outlook should be immediately planted out when there is a certainty that it will soon be cut off by uncontrollable " improvements " on neighboring territory.

The presence of buildings, even crowded together as in cities, by no means necessarily implies an ugly prospect. Many a city back-yard is surrounded by stables, sheds, and tenements which mass in splendid form and composition when seen from one chosen angle or another. Whether in town or country, neighboring buildings may or may not be ugly. The seeing eye must study and know which are good and which bad outlooks, making the garden screens accordingly. The beginning gardener should above all things be free from prejudice. Never assume, " sight unseen," that the neighbor's laundry, waving in the wind, is of necessity objectionable. The glistening white spots may be the only relief from the hopeless monotony of landscape form or color. The artist will always rise above the mere intellectual or moral content of a masterpiece. Gardeners, to be worth the fine title they are gaining for themselves, must be artists, each one as he is able.

Aspect is a different matter. The place should be agreeable to look at from all angles, when finished. The first object in home-building is not, however, to make the place attractive to the neighborhood at the expense of personal comfort or convenience. Our traditions are curiously mixed up and lacking in common sense in respect of these things. Tradition says practically that it makes no difference what is done on a place if only there be an open front lawn on the street side. Thousands of people put almost all their gardening work on the effort to keep the front yard clipped and neat, while they let the side and rear yards run to weeds and trash. This is not worthy of the common sense of the American people. A decent respect for the public is incumbent upon us all. But the honest efforts of a self-respecting man or woman should not all go to putting up a brave front any more than all their money should go on their backs. It is not possible to live at ease in a front yard. So much is obvious. No one would carry a book and a rocking-chair to the front sidewalk to spend a pleasant afternoon. The street side of our small places should be neat and inoffensive. But our work and thought should go to improving and maintaining those parts of our grounds in which we can live in privacy and comfort.

II

ECONOMY IN GROUND–USE

IT would not be surprising in this upside-down modern
world if the next important step in garden design should
be developed in cities and spread to the country. Certainly
one finds in the heart of New York more active interest in
yards that are thoroughly secluded, more an integral part
of the house design and more intensively used, than in our
countryside. City people are learning that an out-of-door
room is a garden even when paved with stone, walled with
brick and concrete, having only such vegetable decoration
as can be grown in pots or boxes. In truth, any enclosed,
sky-covered spot where one likes to live is a garden in the
broad and proper sense. Living must be largely private,
for the Anglo-Saxon at least. Hence the need of enclosure
and seclusion. Our house is still our castle. And the castle,
from which the expression took form, was never without its
" garth " or place to spend the sunny hours outside the cold
forbidding rooms, yet within the fortified area.

The close relation of house and garden, both designed
together within a single enclosure, was retained and developed in France and Italy more than in England, through
which runs the thread of our early American tradition.
Very likely the actual need of defense against marauders
persisted longer on the Continent. Certainly the steel cur-
tains which cover all the lower windows of French shops by
night at the present time show an apprehension that is

inexplicable to the merchant of Chicago. About French homes one finds walls, built on the sidewalk line, which serve to keep the public out as well by day as by night.

Those who have lived in a French city house with a garden, small or large, know that protection against thieves is but an inconsiderable part of a wall's function. Principally it serves to keep the open yard as secluded and as private as indoor living-room and dining-room. French garden walls rise high as prison ramparts, discouraging even curiosity by the dull blank way they face the world. The American traveler on the hustling sidewalk would never guess that within a yard of him sat a woman sewing under a tree, or a baby, untended yet safe from harm among its toys on a bit of green grass. I have spent quiet happy hours in such a tiny court within a hundred yards of the great St.-Lazare railroad station in the heart of Paris. On one side is a marble terrace just large enough for two chairs and a luncheon table, protected by a graceful iron railing. Outside the French window of the jewel-box drawing-room is a flight of three curving steps leading down to a garden of ivy and potted plants. The whole place is smaller than most parlor rugs. Night and day the long windows are left open to the ground. It would be easier for a thief to go in by the second-story window next door than over the walls here. And so ingenious is the arrangement that not a window of the crowded neighborhood can catch a glimpse into this secret garden.

Thus it is that an original function becomes confounded with other advantages which were, perhaps, little considered in the beginning. In landscape design economy on limited land-space is a virtue. The Frenchman sees no sense in paying taxes on land for which neither he nor anyone else gets any return. In this country, from end to end, it would be rare to find a home site, even on the most crowded avenues of our cities, where a bit of land — on which taxes are paid — is not extravagantly, thriftlessly left unused, without compensation in the form of a private garden elsewhere. This is not due to generosity. It expresses thoughtlessness and lack of imagination. The man who will wrestle with his architect over a wasted foot in a bedroom will never stop to think about a larger area wasted out of doors. And in the wasting he will go without what would furnish him with much pleasure — a garden wherein to sit and read and see his friends, as in Paris and in Rome. Is it only the children of old civilizations who have time to study the ramifications of comfort and beauty?

There is every reason to believe that our eyes are now beginning to see beyond the outside walls of our houses, within which we have been content to put our effort and money up to the present time. The garden, as more usually understood, is undergoing a thorough examination, particularly on the part of American women, who are always first in searching out a concrete way toward a more rich and satisfying humanism. For the most part it is they who are improving the yards of their city houses. It may well be they who carry out to their suburbs the memory of the pleasant intimacy of these city outdoor-rooms, which is rarely equaled in the open spaces around country houses, notwithstanding the greater opportunity.

The suburban house on the lot which averages 50 to 75 by 100 feet is usually curiously isolated from the land around it. One feels that a giant might come along any night and change the houses about without making any alteration in the appearance that would be perceptible to the stranger the following day. Most of them would seem to fit equally well on the foundations next door. This is carrying democracy in homes altogether too far. It certainly leads to monotony, which in turn leads to the movies and the automobile-infested roads. But why stay at home in good warm weather when there is nothing but a covered front porch to sit on and no place in which to forget neighbors and public? No, it is up to the American mother to face the existing facts of suburban life and improve the conditions of outdoor home environment, if she wants to find some solution for the nervous urge of the younger generation to be up and away.

And, indeed, that is just what she is trying to do — trying with talk of gardens and flowers. Flower gardens have their place in adding to the pleasures of any home. But, after all, flower gardening appears to the younger generation a rather tame way to spend the time. Yet indoors together they seem to enjoy their cards and gossip and study. Why not give them a place for just such pleasures out of doors, for the summer months, where they can be as independent of prying eyes, as comfortable in heat or cool weather, as free to speak and act, as in the house?

The garden that is needed by the small suburban house might better be called an improvement on the familiar, rather meaningless and useless back-yard. The first thing to do is furnish an easy way to get into it without going out the front door or through the kitchen. Fortunately more and more houses arc being built with a rear verandah, which is a great improvement. If the designer will use a little forethought, he can arrange to extend this verandah by means of an open terrace made of the earth removed from the cellar hole. This was the scheme used by many colonial

From the laundry yard across the width of a small city back-yard, with the next-door house in the background. Economy of use and order in all things make a charming garden of this tiny area.

housebuilders and it is thoroughly practical and economical. Only those who have such a terrace know how pleasant and easy it is to walk out from the house on to the terrace lawn without the interruption of a flight of steps. Such a terrace is the first way and one of the best ways of bringing house and grounds together.

The next move of the man with foresight will be to remove the kitchen and service-windows. At present the back yard is all too apt to focus around the kitchen and laundry. Private garden and cellar stairs, garbage-cans, ash-barrels, and laundry-yard cannot be agreeably mixed up in this country as they sometimes are in Italy. If the back-yard is to be developed into a comfortable extension of the house living-room, the service must be put out of the way, just as it is indoors.

This is not really difficult if we stop a moment to clear our minds of the prejudices and traditions that have lost their meaning because of the changed conditions of modern life. Small houses are even to-day laid out on the schemes first evolved in New England colonial days. In those times people did nothing without a reason. For while they could afford to waste land, they could not afford to waste work, which they had to do themselves or get along without.

Loneliness prompted them to build near together in the towns. They put their houses close to the street, largely to avoid the stupid and needless care we put on our uninteresting front yards to-day. They avoided grass lawns as much as they could. For grass had to be clipped laboriously with a scythe. The lawn-mower is a comparatively new device for saving trouble. In those dull days the only movie was the street, where the footfall of a stranger was enough to set a whole town gossiping. When the hard

work was done the colonial housekeeper liked to move with
her knitting or sewing to the street side of the house, where
she could keep in touch with her small world through the
street window; where she could greet the passing neighbor and run out for a moment to pull a weed and tie up a
rosebush in the garden which lay between house and highway. It was a pleasure to be near the dignified, peaceful
public road.

At the back of the house was the kitchen where she spent
most of her time. For our colonial ancestors had no servants in the early days. They cooked meals and they boiled
soap; they made beer and candles; they spun and wove,
cut clothes and sewed; they washed and scrubbed their
houses, their clothes, and their children; they churned but-
ter; they knitted or "drew" the very rugs on the floor;
they educated their children, did all the work on their
flower gardens, and one day in seven they spent in church.
When we think of them, how wasted and futile seem our
own days, which we like to suppose are profitably busy.
How inexcusable it seems that there should be "no time"
for so many of the things that we know at heart make life
worth while, but never can quite get around to!

Our great-great-grandmother's kitchen was put at the
back of the house because that was the practical place for
it to be. Just outside the kitchen where she spent her time
were the woodshed, the well, the smokehouse, and the short
path to chicken-yards and barns. Between these several
features was a small lawn, used no doubt for children's play
and farm-hands' leisure hours, for a bleaching lawn for flax
and laundry, for the benches full of strawberry preserves,
cooking under the sun. Against the house was a grape
arbor under whose grateful shade she could churn or iron

with one eye on the boiling pot over the open kitchen-fire. The yard was most truly lived in as yards should be. But it saw more work than play. And it was sensible to have it next the kitchen, because it was here that the lady of the house spent most of her waking hours.

Now the churning and the weaving have been forgotten. My lady has more time to sit in her parlor. Some one else does a good part of the cooking, scrubbing, and laundry work. One corner is enough for clothes-yard, ashes, and service. But no one has ever taken the trouble to rearrange the place economically. The clotheslines are scattered anywhere. A garage has gone up in the easiest place — where it belongs in only one case out of ten. The windows of kitchen and pantry look out on a shapeless huddle of divers things of use and ornament, but almost never of beauty. For beauty is found only in order and composition.

These changes within and behind the house are even less striking than what has happened to the public highways. The once quiet broad streets have been filled with a thousand strangers on foot. The silent yoke of oxen is no more. Instead, even minor side streets have been turned into a mad whirlpool of noise, nasty smoke, and rushing Juggernauts. They are fit for nothing but our garages, our service yards, and our backs.

So we come at last to the partial solution of our problem. We must have an attractive house-entrance on the street. But our living-rooms should open on the old despised back-yards now turned into gardens and terraces, no matter how small. The garage should be directly on the street, as is most practical and economical. Kitchen and service-rooms should be on the front, not the back of the house. Laundry-yards should go next the garage, toward the front. If possible, a high wall on the sidewalk line should hide them. Otherwise hedges, shrubberies and other screens should be contrived so that the public, which offends the individual so deeply, shall nevertheless have no cause for complaint. With such a scheme we may be content that not a foot of room has been wasted; that everything is where use and common sense would have it; and that finally we have cleared the old back-yard to make ready for a proper setting for our out-of-door life.

III

OUTDOOR LIVING–ROOMS

WHEN we get the back-yard all to ourselves, what shall we do with it? Personal taste will enter the lists at once. Some will want to fill it with flower beds. Others will call for lawns. Still others will be satisfied only with grapes, fruits, and vegetables. If the place is large enough it can be subdivided to the satisfaction of all. If it is small there must be some compromise. For, like any other general living-room, the whole family must be made comfortable in it, in any event.

Comfort out of doors, in our American climate, calls for a few definite, indispensable things. It requires a place to sit that is well screened against flies and mosquitoes, with a roof to keep out the bugs that drop from above. The endless noisy stinging hosts that attack the unwary, north or south, east or west in this country, do not seem to cause trouble in Europe. At Armenonville in the Bois de Boulogne of Paris, one dines at a table under the trees on the edge of a balustraded lake. It is pleasant to sit there watching the moon rise while swans track the waters at one's feet. Were we able to get all the countryside to combine forces against the vermin of the air, we might have the same pleasure here. And the time will come — has already come in some enlightened communities — to do just this. But complete success is only won slowly here and with never ceasing effort.

While we cannot always be sure of immunity in the open, we can make screened rooms that will be out of doors, yet comfortable and attractive. The usual porch or verandah is more a makeshift than a pleasant room. It is apt to be so narrow that three people and their chairs are crowded unless they sit in an unsociable row with their backs to the wall. Curiously enough, too, porch furniture is usually big and clumsy — much more so than ordinary chairs, without being more comfortable. The addition of a table or plant is apt to clutter up the place badly.

What has proven a pleasant shape indoors will be equally good outdoors. I know of no good rule for the proportions of the living-room of a small house. But it is safe to say that its smallest dimension should be no less than would be livable if the room were square. That is to say, a room fourteen feet square — even twelve feet — is conceivable as a cosy living-room. But a room eight feet square would be impossibly small. Thus, no matter how much longer the room might be, eight feet would be too little for the other dimension of a sitting-room, however well it might do for a hall. The outdoor room should serve the same purpose as the living-room. The rules governing its size are the same. Twelve feet should be the minimum width, and that is satisfactory only with a house so small that the smaller measurement of the living-room is no more. Fourteen feet and more would be better. The length should be as much, or more where practicable. Yet most verandahs are rarely over eight feet wide and thousands of them are not more than six feet! It is only habit that makes such crowding even endurable. Indoors it would not be suffered by anybody for a moment in the smallest flat of the most crowded city. Yet out of doors, where by all the

An outdoor living-room between house and garden. It is brick-paved to keep it cool and screened to keep out insects. It is large enough for real comfort.

laws of fitness one should look for greater freedom, the liberty-loving American stuffs himself into his front porch as he stuffs himself into his automobile — but with far less comfortable upholstery.

The reason is, of course, that the covered verandah is not looked upon as a national necessity, like the indoor living-room, but rather as a temporary need during certain hot hours of the summer months. Yet those hot hours last night and day, for week after week, every year. It is time that the small-house builder should provide something better for himself.

The first objection is apt to come from the architect, who protests that a wide verandah stuck on the side of the typical house makes a monstrous ugly thing. There is no use replying that too few houses are beautiful anyhow. Our small houses are better designed than at any time since the pioneer days. One can, however, easily find precedents in many admirable small houses that have generous outdoor rooms. This detail had better be one condition of the original problem which the architect is given to solve. Of course, he will be plunged into difficulties if the condition be made as an afterthought. It must be studied from the first. If the designer insists that a verandah does not belong on a colonial house, remind him of the old arched woodsheds all over New England, which are one of the most picturesque appointments of the old farm, and can easily be turned into particularly comfortable outdoor living-rooms.

These woodshed-rooms are desirable for two reasons. They are more comfortable than a verandah because they have much more head-room, the floor being on a level with the ground, instead of a couple of feet higher near the level of the first floor of the house. They can easily be made with a large air-chamber between ceiling and roof, which goes far to keep a place cool in hot weather. And since they are on the ground, they are paved with brick or stone built on the cool earth. Not only are they picturesque in themselves, but they serve as an excellent way to " bring the house down to the ground " and thus to make it an intimate part of the landscape design.

The old-fashioned woodshed was connected with the back of the house just where the outdoor living-room is wanted to-day. It is particularly suited to the design that faithfully follows the New England colonial model, whether of town houses like those of Salem or the less pretentious farmhouses. There would be variations for some of the more eclectic recent house-designs. Most of the modern ideas have been inspired by styles found in other parts of the world, where they have been adapted to special local needs by centuries of experience. It may be said with some assurance that the need of an open shed has been common to all men in all places back to the days of barbarism. The architectural student could start out with confidence that he would find picturesque precedents for such a structure in every period and style of human domestic construction.

Successful out-of-door living-rooms have recently been built entirely independent of the house, even some distance away. This scheme offers an added opportunity for the free movement of air, as all four sides may be open to the breezes. Moreover, such a detached structure is really more quiet than is practicable when it is actually a part of the house. Properly screened, it can easily be made a most satisfactory out-of-door sleeping-room, even in thickly inhabited neighborhoods.

The out-of-door living-room, however, must be easily accessible from the house, and easy access means no great change in level between the house floor and the area to be entered. The fact that one must go down three or four steps from the floor of the average house to the ground is probably responsible for the fact that grounds are not more used than they are. In the old Colonial days rarely more than one step separated the kitchen floor and the stone or brick platform just outside the house, where a large part of the summer work was done under the protection of a grape arbor. One step is no hardship for any one to take, even when laden with a considerable burden. Three or four steps are a nuisance to go up and down, and just enough to interfere very much with free access between the two levels. Consequently, it is of the greatest importance to have the ground on the garden side of the house nearly as high as the first-floor rooms. Where the house must be raised above the ground for the sake of the cellar underneath, a terrace of the cellar dirt on the garden side of the house will go far to solve the problem. The outdoor living-room, whether a covered shed (known to architects as a loggia), a verandah, or a semicovered arbor, will be an inviting feature of such a terrace.

Where the house floor is necessarily above the level of the lawn, the terrace will form the most agreeable transition from one to the other. Steps down to the garden level will not drop one from the house doors or attached house-verandahs, but rather they will appear to be stairs in a terrace to let one from a higher to a lower level of the garden. A change in levels between two different areas out of doors can always be made interesting and agreeable. A change of level between the first floor of the house itself and the ground, without modulation from one to the other by means of a terrace, sets the building apart from the garden and lawn in a way that is unfortunate both for appearance and for use.

Indeed, the key to the real use of the garden area by the whole family will depend on easy accessibility from the house rooms and on finding a comfortable place to sit and live out of doors when they get out, well screened from neighbors.

IV

LAWNS — GREEN GARDENS

The American caller in England is apt to be surprised, on being told that his hostess is " in the garden," to find her under a tree on the lawn. A well-arranged small lawn is a garden. Something is wrong with it otherwise. Yet American lawns rarely inwite one to linger. They are usually indeterminate areas covered with grass, into which house, drives, and gardens are dropped down like a few fishballs on a large platter.

A good lawn must be enclosed by buildings, walls, or planting, as a general thing — exceptionally by lake, ocean, or river — on one or more sides. Open landscape and distant views embellish a good lawn from which they can be seen. But fairly strong demarcation between the two is better if intimacy is, as it should be, a strong consideration. A small enclosed lawn is an out-of-door room, susceptible of treatment as varied as any indoor apartment.

On a small place, the house usually forms one boundary; the property-line marks one or even all the other three. In other places the hedge or wall, shutting out flower gardens or service buildings, completes the frame.

The boundaries of the small lawn constitute not only its walls, but also most of its decoration. Planting, of course, plays a major part and here skillful use of shrubs and trees is particularly important. One commonly sees monstrous banks of bushes with slightly wiggled outlines as stiff as old-fashioned bed-bolsters, to which period of artistic achievement they properly belong. They are composed of elongated cellular groups of, say, six *Forsythia suspensa,* eight *Lonicera morrowi,* five lilacs, seven *Philadelphus grandiflorus* "faced down" by seven *Spiræa vanhouttei,* nine Japanese barberry, and twelve *Symphoricarpus* in the shade. Miles of these and similar shrub-combinations are still being planted from the impetus given by late-Victorian models in such matters. Their chief virtue is that they form definite — if uninteresting — walls of foliage. They lack fine quality in silhouette, texture, light and shade. The thing is better done by chance along any overgrown farm-fence or wall.

Such combinations are too logical. They are like scientific classifications in which shrubs, trees, flowers, and ferns are dealt with each by each. Nature has a way of mixing things up. She is more apt to line up a tree, two tall bushes, a clump of fern, a rock, another tree — and better so. Take a leaf out of such a planting-book in composing the lawn borders. Remember, too, that Nature's best effects are always a phase in the war for the survival of the fittest. Overplant everywhere, mixing up varieties of many things, with a preponderance of two or at most three varieties from among the many used.

More explicitly assume that a narrow boundary-planting two hundred feet long is being planned around a lawn. Plant one hundred trees and shrubs (far more — perhaps ten to twenty times more — that can develop to their individual advantage). Assuming that a sunny area is wanted, not more than three trees can be permitted to grow large. Plant six to ten of one or at most two varieties. There is a permanent place for six small trees, such as hawthorns, flowering crabs, Japanese tree-lilacs or flowering dogwood. Plant ten of one variety, three of a second, and two of a third. From year to year one or more of the superfluous trees can be taken out, when they have had time to show unmistakably which will be the best specimens.

If one has ten years or so to wait for shrubs to grow to their full height and spread, half a dozen large ones would fill in the gaps. Many shrubs cover a circle from fifteen to twenty-five feet in diameter if given room and opportunity. But this takes too long for the average person. Instead of six, plant sixty and more shrubs, half large, half small. Shrubs are considered large or small roughly according to their condition after four or five years' growth in any given neighborhood. For instance, *Philadelphus grandiflorus* normally is said to be a ten-foot shrub, to which height it rather quickly grows. Old plants are not uncommonly much taller. Japanese barberry is thought of as a low shrub with a four-foot maximum height. It grows to be eight feet high in time.

As with the trees, the bulk of both large and small shrubs should be of one or two varieties with a few odd sorts for variety and accent. Here and there among the shrubs should be scattered perennials like *Cimicifuga*, which appear at their best isolated, or clumps of foxgloves, Michælmas daisies, or ferns, and ground-cover of *Sedum stoloniferum*, Christmas roses, *Vinca minor* or *Veronica rupestris*. Endless changes in the combinations of plant materials for border plantations are available in native and imported varieties. In every case, however, all types and sizes of things should be included unless a frank hedge is more appropriate.

Hedges themselves are susceptible of a much more varied

treatment than one usually sees. Most people again are cramped by logic. They make hedges of one plant-variety only. Privet, Japanese barberry, box, are within everybody's imaginative compass. From time to time one sees Osage orange, Japanese quince, buckthorn, hawthorn, beech, white pine, hemlock, arborvitæ or Norway spruce in long clipped lines. Each is admirable in its place. But why be limited? There are few shrubs or trees which will not thrive under the discipline of the shears. Some of them, like *Spiræa vanhouttei*, show new and unexpected qualities when clipped. Their peculiar beauty lies in the grace of their untrammeled growth. But we have opportunity to observe that fact in unnumbered millions of examples throughout the land. A few hundred can well be spared to make fine hedges here and there.

In still other places many a small-lot owner whose shrub plantations are growing too wide will discover that good clipped hedges can be made of mixed varieties of shrubs. They may not have the machine-made stiffness of California privet, but they have a more interesting texture and otherwise are quite as effective. Many trees, like the European beech, normally branch to the ground and can make part of the mixed hedge. When once a tree has lost its lower branches, however, it is difficult if not impossible to force others to grow from the bottom of the trunk.

One virtue of the mixed hedge lies in the fact that it can be clipped on one side, next a path, for instance, and allowed to grow naturally on the other side, next an open lawn, with better effect than a single variety gives. Wherever possible, even on very small places, advantage should be taken of this fact to make a path through the border plantation, at least on one side or end of the lawn if not all about. These border paths can be made among the most attractive of all the landscape features. In one place they will lie between a high hedge on one side and low flowering bushes on the other. Elsewhere they will tunnel under tall branches. They will open on to a simple arbor for grapes and wistaria which harbors a comfortable bench. They will widen a bit where the path is edged with bulbs and perennials. Under a tall tree's shade will be ferns and a bird bath, well out of reach of marauding cats. In the corner behind thick foliage will be a shed — small and shallow — for flat tools, each on its special hook or peg. From one end to the other of the lawn-border planting this path can give a constant pleasure, whether through variety of treatment and little surprises on a winding path, or the simple harmonious dignity of continuous arbor or straight clipped hedge.

Whatever is done, the border treatment of both sides of the lawn must be well harmonized and balanced. It is twice as hard to get an agreeable result with a stiff clipped hedge on one side and an informal hedgerow on the other, as it would be in a room with different wall-paper on opposite walls. It is better to continue with hedges if you start with them. Then the interest in the lawn will depend on its shape, decoration, and accent.

Any shaped lawn enclosed by a clipped hedge is necessarily definite and obvious. Consequently, that shape must be agreeably proportioned or the result will be ugly. Humanity has agreed after experimenting that a few shapes are almost fool-proof. The circle and the square are admittedly unimpeachable. Rectangles may or may not be agreeable shapes, and here good taste must be the popular rule. Converging lines and formal curves not segments

of circles are more apt to be bad than good and should
be avoided by the amateur, who will find plenty of variety to exercise his imagination in working with circles
or parts of circles, and squares or rectangles, alone or in
combinations.

Definite geometrical areas, which are the result of this
process, require softening or they become stiff dead things.
The most welcome relief for lawns is found in deep irregular
shadow, such as falls away from tall trees.   The trees
should stand to the east, south, or west, rather than north,
to get the best results.   Sometimes they are found within
the lawn area, a pleasant accident.

The shapes of informally bordered lawns are not so easily
classified by the average person and hence not apt to offend.
Like others, they may be good, bad, or merely dull.   But
their satisfactory treatment depends on a knowledge of
" occult balance " — whether consciously and technically or
not — and this is the result of experience and observation,
not of rule.

A good lawn is a Green Garden.   But it is only one kind
of green garden.   True lovers of plants and gardens, as
distinguished from mere floriculturists, interest themselves
more and more in green gardens.   In them form, texture,
and quiet color of vegetation can be studied without dis-
traction.   The green garden is par excellence a place of
serenity and repose.   At best, it is a place of cool color.
Flowers are not banished.   They are incidental merely,
accenting seasons or throwing a shadow into prominence.
Hot red, orange, yellow, green, and purple should be
avoided.

The green garden is particularly adapted to the needs
of a small place.   It can be designed so as to require a

minimum of time and work to maintain. It needs little more than a restraining, guiding hand. Most of the real work can be done over a teacup in the shade. It is done in the mind. One decides, " The clump of pines is too heavy. It needs a canoe birch in the foreground "; or, " The *Rhododendron carolinianum* looks too like a setting hen over that boulder. A drooping *Leucothoë catesbei* would be better. The red stems of the rhododendron leaves would look well in the corner near the red-twigged cornel bushes "; or, " The shade is too dense here where the flickering sunlight used to play on the grass. The oak will be all the better for cutting out some of the upper branches. Which ones will have to go? " or, " The bush honeysuckle has grown too big for this little place. A large-leaf shrub would be a bull in a china shop. It's just the place for two or three graceful inkberry (*Ilex glabra*) with their shiny evergreen leaves. In front a carpet of bearberry (*Arctostaphylos uva-ursi*) might prosper in my mean, sandy, acid soil."

The real work in a green garden consists of endless searching and questioning, and comparatively little physical labor. It is the sort of place about which the flower enthusiast will say: " What a sweet peaceful spot! Why don't you put in some flower beds? It's a pity not to make a garden here."

In many places the floor of the green garden will be planted with turf. But grass is used far more than necessary. A curious notion prevails that sowing grass is the only way to cover the ground except where there are beds of shrubs or flowers. Yet our hot dry summers make it very difficult to get good lawns.

Close examination usually shows that grass is only one and sometimes a scarce plant in lawns. It is rather silly to keep up the old delusion, under the circumstances. There are a host of plants which make admirable ground-covers. Many of them take no care save for a little weed-ing. A few of them will stand being walked upon con-stantly. Unless one likes to run a lawn-mower, it is far better and often prettier to cover the ground with other plants. A little study will show where grass is needed — for sunny paths, around the tea table under the trees where the shade is not too heavy, or on the terrace where one walks and sits.

The wise gardener, economical of work, will plan to let mats of other plants push the grass lawns away from the corners and the beds. The material used will depend on circumstances, of course. Where one wishes to walk from time to time, the mouse-eared or the small-leaved thyme will thrive on a hot dry bank or rocks; *Veronica rupestris,* *V. repens,* mosslike *Arenaria* will quickly spread over good soil; mosses, moneywort (*Lysimachia nummularia*) will grow in the shade. Where there is no need to walk, the possible variety of plants is legion. Myrtle (*Vinca minor*), *Pachysandra terminalis,* bugle (*Ajuga reptans*), partridge berry (*Mitchella repens*), *Arenaria montana,* violets, *Gyp-sophila repens,* the lycopodiums, *Phlox subulata,* sedums, and so on, will thrive, some in sun, others in shade.

The study of form and composition in terms of vege-tation is especially fruitful in the green garden because of the slow rhythm of growth. Herbaceous plants come in a day and go in a night. They are difficult for the landscape picture-maker to arrange, save as he is satisfied with chang-ing flower color. Texture and form of herbaceous plants in combination are but lightly touched upon by amateurs. The material of the green garden moves more slowly.

Trees, shrubs, ground-cover, and incidental groups of taller herbaceous plants are susceptible of leisurely study. They vary but little from month to month and from one year to the next. This growth can be pushed or retarded by individualized treatment. Consequently the green-garden maker becomes especially sensitive to the refinements of plant life. He is the sculptor of a never finished statue. In Japan, where patience in artistic achievement is developed with more than Occidental stoicism, trees are kept dwarf for generations because of their especial fitness for some minor garden-effect. Few Americans will follow their example. But the reason will be understood by the green gardener now and again, when he would like to keep forever a bit of skyline silhouette, or the vertical lines of a red cedar clump where they just balance the horizontal branches of the flowering dogwood.

Obviously size plays no part in such intensive studies. The gardener with a dozen growing things can work for perfection which the master of a thousand acres cannot hope to rival, for attention to detail is only possible in few things. The size of the canvas has never been the measure of great painting.

Similarly, a real interest in plant textures is stimulated by intensive work on a small place. Good taste in foliage texture lags behind good taste in the texture of dress goods. But it is equally important. The kitchen apron must not be of satin nor overalls of red velvet. Yet, because of ignorance, such blunders are constantly committed in gardens. Petunias and nasturtiums are grown on gaunt native ledges. Begonias edge beds of absurdly clumped evergreens. Salvia is everywhere. Little houses are belted with bulging shrubs as mud rolls out from under a footfall. In connection with architecture, bad taste in the size, form, and texture of vegetation is particularly apparent. As in matters of dress, good taste depends on common sense and knowledge of the right thing in the right place. Experiments in the green garden will soon show one what is right and what is wrong, as harmonies and discords are obvious. The thoughtful student will soon see that Boston ivy smothers a sundial or the carved posts of an entrance porch, when a delicate ivy that can be pruned easily, such as *Ampelopsis aconitifolia* could be made to festoon, but never hide its support; or that horse-chestnuts close to a house with their heavy mats of foliage make the rooms dark and gloomy, while locust trees, which are but little more dirty, let light and air through. Such examples of texture are for him who runs to read. But in all other details, both practical and æsthetic, similar selection and discrimination will become absorbingly interesting to the gardener of the green garden.

The repose of a green garden deserves a bit of emphasis. Too many flower-gardens become slave drivers. Their owners never dare sit down in them. Weeds spring up while the back is straightening. Faded flowers forever call for the scissors. Late or diseased larkspur or phlox must be doctored, cuddled, and worried over. At its best, they have a dangerous tendency to resemble the White Queen's condiment in *Through the Looking Glass*, "Jam to-morrow and jam yesterday — but never jam to-day."

Not so with the green garden. It may have its great moments when the hawthorn is in bloom or the maple turns red in the autumn. Otherwise it is a cool quiet green place, rarely drawing attention to itself, but content to be, like a dim, old room full of books — a place to live and think, and perhaps at times to dream.

V

THE FLOWER GARDEN

THE flower garden, to be a garden, must have a good background on at least three sides, eye high. Beyond that, the rules are almost free for all to make. Nowhere do personal preferences show more strongly than for types and kinds of flower gardens. If properly designed and carried out, anything may be good. If poorly or insufficiently conceived ahead of time, nothing will be good. This does not mean that everything must be foreseen. Some of the best gardens have grown and been added unto year after year, quite without conscious plan on the part of the designer. Indeed, such an one is rather apt to boast — just a trifle — that it was done without any plan whatever. He or she may not realize it, but this is poppycock. On inquiry, it will come out that the garden problem has been studied in great detail; that ten little schemes have been rejected to one that has been carried out; that experiments have been tried and changed when they did not work; that, most important of all, the gardener has strong likes and dislikes on the subject of gardens. This means a thoroughgoing philosophy of gardening and garden design, even where there has been no technical training whatever. Experience is still a good school where coupled with quick observation of other people's successes and failures.

There are three rules, however, that must be obeyed at peril of failure. Soil must be right. Fertilizers must be applied. There must be water. The first two are one in theory, but two in practice.

Americans home from England are all too apt to credit the brilliantly successful gardens there to the favorable climate. At least seventy-five per cent of the secret is not climate, but work. The Englishman takes out the soil of a new flower-bed three feet deep; puts in drains at the bottom, and laboriously refills with good loam and fertilizer. Moreover, he repeats this process in the same beds when they " run out." How many Americans take such trouble? Yet here it is the more necessary if our climate is a handicap, as it surely is in some regions. Far better do a small bed well each year than many beds poorly for supposed immediate effect.

The average person seems to like flower gardens that are formal, but not stiff. Definite forms and shapes appeal to the normal sense of order. Instinctively we make our paths straight and our beds regular. Such a garden is undeniably simplest to maintain. We think too little about tying the landscape organization of the whole place together by means of our straight garden paths. They are apt to begin and go nowhere. By organization is meant that all details and parts of a place must be in proper relation to each other and to the whole, as in a house the living-room opens on to hall, dining-room on to living-room, and kitchen on to dining-room, all the rooms together forming the organization plan of the house. The parts of a place are tied together when their relationship to each other is made apparent.

In old colonial houses we frequently find that a straight path leads from the street to the front door, where one can see through the middle of the house and out the garden door. Further beyond began the central garden-path, which continued out to the end of the place. Thus, in many good colonial examples, balanced front-yard, house-plan and garden-plan were all strung like beads on one straight string, which is called the axis. This is a simple and agreeable scheme on which to build the small garden to-day.

The central hall has rather gone out of fashion in houses, and in its absence some other definite feature should be selected from which to draw out the garden path: the steps or door of a rear verandah, the entrance or centre of an outdoor living-room, or the principal window of the house on the garden side. This is more important than to have the two sides of the garden symmetrical, which can be easily compromised if the path does not happen to lie in the obvious middle of the garden.

There are ways of recognizing an axis without a path. A formal oblong grass-panel, at the far end of which the interest is focalized in a gate, arbor, or other object, will serve just as well. Sometimes it is possible to leave an opening between trees and, at the far end of the otherwise unmarked axis, put a conspicuous well-head or bird-bath. It is hardly worth while to make a catalogue of various possible treatments of axes, which should in every case be made to fit the peculiar conditions of any new garden as they are revealed. The important point is to remember the axis when planning the garden — to decide more or less definitely where to put it and what to do with the near end or entrance and the far end or visual terminus of the future garden. Then the intermediate area will more or less look out for itself. One needs to remember only to keep an unobstructed view from one end of the axis to the other.

The principle of the axis depends, in analysis, on the natural and human desire that there be a beginning and an end of a work of art — which a garden must be. It promises also that somehow we can get from where we are to what we see in the distance. An open path is the simple fulfilment of this promise. But there is no principle of design requiring so blunt a solution of the traffic problem.

The garden is not a place to rush through as quickly as possible. It should tempt one to leisurely progress from one to another pleasant feature. The headlong visitor may need a curb. There is no harm in making the paths quite roundabout on the way to the garden's end. In paths, practical convenience must be the criterion of the small gardener. If — because of a steep slope or other natural obstruction — it will promote ease of maintenance to carry the paths at an angle across the place from end to end or around the sides, the final effect is apt to be the more charming.

For convenience' sake, it is necessary to get across the garden as well as from end to end. The principle of axial arrangement holds on cross-views and paths in a minor way. They should have a beginning and an end. Where cross-paths meet lengthwise paths one is inclined to elaborate the intersections by enlargement into little squares or circles or by marking with conspicuous plants at the four corners.

At least the main through path of the garden should be wide enough for two people to walk abreast. It is astonishing how little this fact seems to be generally realized. In all common sense the beds and decoration are but to enhance the path, the place where people go to enjoy other things. Walking single file, sometimes even having to pick one's way between overhanging bushes and flowers, is a poor way to enjoy companionship. Yet in most of our gardens the paths are narrow and the beds wide, as though the paths were the lesser things. A clear four-feet is the narrowest width for the comfortable passage of two people. If nothing is planted where it will overhang the walking space, even when fully developed, a four-foot path is enough for the small garden. But where plants, hedges, or bushes are to be allowed to sprawl as they will, greater width will be needed from the first. Evem in a small garden, nothing short of six feet should be set apart for such a walk.

When the place is first laid out, this will seem enormous. That is to be expected. Wait only a few weeks. If trailing nasturtiums, *Nepeta mussini,* or any other rather sprawly plant has been put at the path's edge, it will be necessary before the first summer's end to begin to cut back the encroaching stems.

The material of which paths should be made is largely determined by their use. Ordinary grass paths are quickly ruined by heavy wheelbarrows and are too wet for comfort after a rain, or with the dew on them; they are not easy to keep level and even in quality. The grass roots persist in getting into the flower beds at the sides and a maximum effort is required to keep them well weeded and the edges cut. They are by all odds most costly to maintain in good condition. But they are pleasant to look at and to use in good weather.

Common earth-walks are either muddy or dusty, but there are many kinds of surfacing gravels and crushed stone that can be used to advantage on a good foundation. The technical value of color is almost the only criterion, once admitting that the texture must be agreeable underfoot. Diffcrent materials can be bought, from the gleaming white

of oyster shells and the creamy silver of beach pebbles,
through the cold grays of crushed trap-rock or the browns,
yellows, pinks, and reds of varicolored stone to jet black
anthracite coal. Often the available local material deter-
mines the color. Indeed, it is sometimes amusing to see,
in the gardens of people who would be horrified at the mere
idea of using " colored stones " in their gardens, walks that
are bright yellow, pink, or red, because of the gravel found
in their neighborhood.

Paths play an important part in giving character to the
garden. To make it brilliant one uses light-colored gravel
which matches in color value the bright flowers or gay-
leaved plants, hiding the dark foliage of other things as
much as possible. To get richness one uses a medium-dark
gravel and the strong green of box and rhododendrons, for
instance, interspersed with light green ferns and strong
masses of flowers in cooler tones. To get quiet even mix-
tures we use dark — even black — gravel, dull gray-green
yew and Douglas spruce, accentuated with an occasional
clump of strong-growing flowers. In all such arrangements
the color of the paths is important as the color of floors
and walls is important in the house.

For other uses and effects walks are made of brick, tile,
stone, concrete, or combinations of these materials. Brick
is a favorite stuff for walks in this country. Custom alone
— certainly not common sense — makes a bright pink or
red brick really seem restrained and conservative to people
who would shudder at using the same colors in any other
material. Pressed or glazed brick should be avoided. It
is monotonous in color and slippery when wet. The best
brick is well burned, but varied in color and shape and
slightly porous. It may be laid with wide joints which

will fill with moss if properly treated. The final tone is sumptuous and quiet.

A little thought given to the other materials will determine whether stone, tile, or concrete would be even better under certain circumstances than brick, crushed stone, or gravel. The ordinary granolithic walk is of course an abomination to the eye with its hard, monotonous, uninteresting, yet insistent color and texture. A concrete walk need not be ugly, but it generally is.

Details of planting do not lie within the province of this short study. But it is wise to caution the beginning gardener that many, many flower gardens are spoiled because they have too many flowers. A series of beds of flowers alone is a monotonous sight at best, though they may be astonishing as bright floricultural "stunts." Just as occasional flowers should be put in the border shrub- and tree-plantations, so should incidental trees and shrubs be mingled with the flowers in the beds.

For one thing, certain shrubs — such as old fashioned flowering almond — and trees — such as flowering crabs, cherries, plums — far exceed any known herbaceous or annual plants in the splendor and mass of their flowers. In the second place, many garden flowers are to be seen at their best only against immediate backgrounds and in composition with taller growing things. Some grow more successfully among the roots of trees and shrubs. In the third place, and as reason enough in itself, the taller shrubs and trees break up the sky line; they throw shadows here and there, without which a parterre becomes an arid waste; and they relieve the borders of rigidity. They give the garden "atmosphere." Better far, if necessary, sacrifice some of the perfection of individual bloom to this intangible quality without which no garden is much better than a florist's exhibition.

Flower beds may be regularly planted with exact repetition of material at definite and obvious intervals; with less marked rhythm in which masses or colors are repeated; or with a tangle of flowers in which the repetitions lose all apparent relationship.

The first method is regaining popularity which it lost because it was badly done over a long period. At its worst it is known as carpet-bedding. Of such were flower beds during the sixties and seventies of the last century when stars, circles, and crescents were stuffed with conspicuous plants in ugly, grotesque combinations. Huge caladium and canna leaves burst from wretched lines of coleus, ice plant, and houseleeks. Wholesale condemnation is a dangerous thing, especially in matters of taste. Because carpet-bedding was bad, the world jumped to the conclusion that all planting done with regular patterns must necessarily be ugly and stiff. It took a long time for people to realize that under certain circumstances nothing but this type of design was appropriate, especially in formal gardens which had any flavor of the French style. During the long discussion of carpet-bedding and formal design versus herbaceous borders and informal design, the French have gone their own way. They have followed their own genius for order even when dealing with our familiar herbaceous plants. As a result the French flower beds are chic and almost inimitable. Of course they are at times frankly open to question on the part of the American. They have startling color combinations. For instance, one sees whole beds of dwarf crimson ramblers edged with brilliant yellow calceolarias. In this country we have no gray cold stone walls and gray days which make this sort of composition endurable as in Paris. On the other hand, some of their planting schemes are effective and can be used in the smallest garden where classic order best serves the interests and desires of the owner. Their beds of regular width alongside a path, for instance, are often edged with dwarf box. The centre line of the bed is marked by standard lilacs, roses, heliotrope, or lantana, repeated at regular intervals of from five to ten feet. Between these will be broken lines of other plants. The best bedding I remember was arranged in lines as follows: —

1. Box edging
2. Alternate ageratum and Souvenir de Bonn abutilon
3. Pink begonia
4. Whitish pink begonia interrupted by one yellow calceolaria every fifth plant
5. Red begonia and ageratum alternately
6. (Middle line) standard roses 10 feet apart: halfway between, one large yellow calceolaria — the rest heliotrope

5, 4, 3, 2, 1 repeated

As time goes on I believe that the development of honesty among gardeners — which means always a growth of individual taste — will reveal the fact that many people are really fond of this classic sort of garden design, just as many people are fond of classic austerity and fine proportion in houses, even where it can be gotten only at the expense of coziness. Gardening will be the better for the development of all sorts of ideas in garden design.

The best herbaceous borders in the American sense generally are made with certain repetitions of masses and colors, between which is put a variety of other plants.

Sometimes these masses are easily recognized, as when a group of hollyhocks is repeated at fifteen-foot intervals, subdivided by Shasta daisies or white Jeanne d'Arc phlox in their own season. This repetition becomes slightly less obvious when the form of growth is not quite so distinct as in hollyhocks.

Where one desires to get away from the regularity of repeated groups of the same color, the rhythm can be maintained less obviously by using different colors of the same plant. Between these major groups of plants lesser things may or may not be regularly repeated. On the whole, it is probably better to keep four or five well-recognized plants in regular relation to each other. There will be sufficient variety given by the " fillers in " between these groups to do away with any sense of rigidity, while the repetitions will keep the whole bed in harmonious relationship.

Many people are fond of a tangle of flowers, in which there is hardly any appreciable repetition at definite intervals. There are few gardeners, however, who do not realize that, on the whole, taller plants must be kept more or less away from the edges of the beds if we are to see the lower growing things. Obviously, hollyhocks next to the path will make it impossible to see — and consequently absurd to plant — snapdragon or browallia in the middle of the bed.

Color composition in flower beds has been much studied and written about during the past few years, which is an excellent thing. Amateurs should be warned against laying too much emphasis on details of color combinations, however, as one is sure to be often disappointed. Flowers have a way of refusing to blossom when they are expected, of growing taller or shorter than previous experience led one

*A Little Garden next the house, formal in plan but not stiff,
because of a nice sense of loose yet orderly composition in plants.
This garden was done entirely by the mind and hands of the
owner, who spends most of her time painting pictures.*

to suppose they would. Sometimes, because of the weather, flowers come and go within a fortnight's time which should have spread their season over six weeks or two months. This throws all flower combinations decidedly out of gear. The arrangement of flowers in the beds should be carefully worked out very much as the positions of chairs and tables should be carefully arranged in rooms. Then, as time goes on, one must not be put out if certain things do not look just as they should, but have to be moved one way or the other.

Painters realize better than gardeners that, given a sufficient volume, all flower colors may be mingled with impunity. While one would hate to see very much pink phlox against orange-yellow helenium, yet one or two such accidents make a refreshing variation in a large and otherwise well-ordered bed. Whereas these two, or many other combinations, are almost intolerable if examined as a detail, they take their places as insignificant brilliant spots when the whole garden is seen in a broad way. If women have a fault in gardening it is that they are more apt to be interested in these little details than in the general effect. Overattention to little details will make them perfect, but, curiously enough, it is more apt to mean an indifferent parterre or series of garden beds. This is true of gardens devoted to one color. Blue gardens or pink gardens are rarely successful because of overrefinement; moreover, many of our favorite plants are necessarily omitted when the planting is limited to one general color.

In a broad way one may say that yellows, especially bright yellows, are most satisfactory in springtime, when the narcissus, crocus, and tulip turn the snow to gold. In midsummer bright yellow is a hot color and should be avoided. Pale straw-color and lemon yellow, however, are delightful midsummer colors, as they seem to stay cool and sparkle — especially in late afternoon, when they almost exactly match in color the yellow rays of the setting sun on green leaves. In the autumn birches lead the way again to exquisite yellow, when it becomes one of the most beautiful colors of the season, in harmony with all changing foliage.

Blue and violet are excellent garden colors from the beginning to the end of the season. Pink, in contrast with yellow, should start soft in the springtime and strengthen in tone to a climax in pink roses. After the early summer it is almost always more beautiful if turned slightly toward salmon. A clear true pink in August and September seems quite out of harmony with the somewhat faded, dull foliage-greens, and in late autumn it looks out of place.

Red at present is one of the rather unpopular garden colors. Probably it is because it overbalances more delicate hues, especially when used in quantity. Moreover, red is an insistent color with which it is fairly difficult to harmonize other subtle shades. At times nothing will take its place. It is complementary to foliage greens: a useful fact to know. Reds of course have tendencies either toward scarlet and orange, or toward crimson and purple. These two kinds of red do not fraternize with any success. In choosing a red flower one must take pains to study the other colors that are to be used in the immediate neighborhood.

Magenta is one of the fundamental flower-colors of Nature to which half of the flower kingdom reverts when it gets a good chance. Unfortunately, magenta flowers are almost never in harmonious relation to the green foliage of their own plants. Moreover, they are most apt to come toward the end of the season when the world begins to turn brown and yellow. Magenta combines but ill with such colors. That is the real reason why magenta is so particularly unpopular. It is a beautiful color in the spring with the bright green grass. Later in the year, if the dull green foliage can be hidden with silver or gray leaves, magenta flowers will often be exceptionally pretty in flower beds, especially where they lie — part of the time at least — in the shade.

THE CUT-FLOWER, VEGETABLE, AND FRUIT GARDEN

THERE is every reason to supplement the green garden or even the flower garden itself with a place for cut flowers and vegetables. It may well be that the artist who is not tied down by prejudices will see no reason why border plants, cut-flower plants, and even vegetables should be put in different places. From the standpoint of the practical gardener, however, there is a definite reason for doing so. The good designer will follow both artist and practical gardener. Cut flowers should be so grown as to make the most satisfactory bloom for cutting to put in house vases. The ordinary flower garden from which flowers are removed in quantities oftentimes suffers a good deal in appearance. Consequently, it is desirable at times, especially in the small flower garden, to be able to leave the flowers where they are for their decorative quality out of doors, rather than in.

Moreover, in growing plants for their flowers alone, it is easier to get the best results with the least work by keeping them in lines like vegetables, rather than in mixed groups, as must ordinarily be done in the flower garden. Because they are grown like vegetables it is often easiest to put them where they can be weeded, tilled, and watered, with radishes, lettuce, and other smaller vegetables.

A good many of them have only a short season during which they look really well, and perhaps a long season before and after when they are shabby. Such plants are unsatisfactory in the flower garden, although oftentimes we cannot spare them altogether. A few plants, like mignonette, have a growth that is sprawly and weak most of the time. It is much better to put all this sort of material more or less by itself, where it can be easily taken care of and will at the same time make an interesting show of flowers at one season or another.

While a small lot is not a satisfactory place on which to grow large vegetables, yet enough fresh peas, beets, beans, lettuce, radishes, and even green corn can be grown in a small area to feed a family of four, if the quantities and rotation are intelligently studied.

In Italian farm-gardens no distinction is made between flowers and vegetables — especially flowers and decorative vegetables, of which there are many. There is reason on the small place in putting some of the vegetables in the actual flower-borders. No foliage is finer than that of the red pepper and as a bit of color the fruit has a beauty that cannot be replaced by any garden flower. For a small garden-bed there is no reason why an edging of parsley would not be as pretty and as satisfactory as anything else. Sometimes knowing gardeners make flower-bed edgings of chives, which, with their neat foliage and pretty pink flowers, always draw forth surprised enthusiasm from less wise ones who may be growing yards of it outside the flower garden without ever having given it a thought. Other vegetables are notable for beauty of color, but many of them are not particularly satisfactory in flower beds. For instance, the grays, blues, and violets of cabbage and cauliflower are quite without peers in the world of flower color. But, in order to get any satisfactory results from them as vegetables, they have to be grown as individual specimens. The great leaves and superb flowering stalks of the ordinary rhubarb are worth growing as flowering plants if some place can be found for them where their shabby appearance at the end of the season will not be objectionable.

Among the best of our annual vines are the scarlet-runner bean and lima bean, which, with their fine foliage and their useful fruit, might often be grown with great success where a decorative annual vine is wanted. They certainly would be more successful than the average plants of *Cobœa scandens*, which is the more ordinarily used decorative annual vine for late-season work. As a tremendously rampant grower with fine blue-gray foliage, nothing could exceed the splendor of a well-grown Himalayan blackberry.

While the flowering fruit trees, crab apples, peaches, cherries, and plums are among the finest decorative plants that have ever been introduced into gardens, most of them suffer from having only one " season," namely, that in which they are in flower. The real fruiting trees of similar sorts are in many cases equally beautiful when in flower and when in fruit.

The natural inference on the small place will be, of course, " Why not put these useful plants in place of other trees and shrubs where decorative material is wanted? " Nothing could be better. Of course, where shrubs and trees are grown for decorative effect as well as for their fruit, they will have to be put in among other trees and bushes and grown in a way that will not bring about perfect fruit. Nevertheless, the quantity and quality of the fruit from crab apples, quinces, cherries, pears, plums, and so on which are grown in hedgerows and boundary plantings are sufficiently good to make them of real value to the householder. Fortunately, too, all this material is reasonably small in its final growth, so that it is easy to give it a place on a fairly small lot. The largest of all is probably the fully developed apple-tree. Nothing could be finer to live under than an old apple-tree. If, however, there is too little space for one, it is possible now to get dwarf apple trees of almost any size down to the very smallest. Where even the smallest tree is undesirable, one can still use cordon fruits. Cordons are fruit trees that are allowed to grow only about two feet high, trained to grow along wires, so that they make attractive little hedges. The finest fruit is to be obtained at times in surprisingly large quantities from such little cordon fruit-trees, and it would be difficult to find a more delicate and interesting hedge than they make. Their flowers in the spring and their blushing fruit in the autumn put them in a class that is suitable for the flower garden or along any walk of the place. Where a heavier hedge is wanted, but still something that is low, consider the currant. For the beauty of its foliage it is exceeded by nothing short of the similar Western sumac, *Rhus trilobata*, which does not seem to thrive very well in the East. Yet the currant is seldom found among decorative shrub-plantations.

The almost equally decorative gooseberry could be used for a prickly hedge. It is quite as handsome as the Japan barberry. Of course, currants and gooseberries cannot be planted nowadays in regions where the white pine is a valuable tree, because of the white-pine blister-rust, which travels back and forth between the *ribes* and the five-needled pines.

Where a still taller hedge is wanted, especially around

a cut-flower and vegetable garden, — which should be enclosed like any other garden, — one can use raspberries and
blackberries for an effective way of keeping people where
they belong.

A little study from unprejudiced observation of many
so-called useful plants will show that they may be made
equally important from a decorative point of view. No
tree could be more satisfactory in a wide flower-bed than
a quince with its exquisite pink flowers in the spring and
fine lemon-yellow fruit in the autumn. It has a picturesque
habit of growth at all seasons.

On the other hand, a good many of the decorative plants
which are, supposedly, otherwise useless will be found most
useful when experiments are made. For instance, the Japanese quince often bears fruit that makes quite as good jelly
as the fruiting quince. At the same time, of course, it makes
an admirable hedge. It is susceptible to scale, but this
pest can be kept down by spraying. It is unrivaled for
gorgeous salmon and orange-red flowers in the springtime
and proves to be a most awkward hedge to get through.

Nowadays the wild-barberry fruit is rarely used to make
jelly, but, up to a short time ago, it was considered to be
one of the regular kitchen-supply plants like the currant.
I have never heard of the Japan barberry being used for
jelly and, while the wild barberry is under a shadow at the
moment, notwithstanding its beauty, — because it harbors
wheat rust, — yet it is a pretty, useful shrub.

These indications are enough to show how important it
is for the small householder to observe carefully the appearance of useful plants and the fruiting qualities of decorative
plants when it comes to the decoration and arrangement
of the place. Of course, on the other hand, it is exceedingly

important that mistakes should not be made. Some garden
favorites are poisonous. There is no need to warn people
against poison ivy and poison dogwood. Most people know
that aconite or monkshood is dangerous. Some few other
popular plants are unwholesome, if not dangerous, to either
man or animals, and care should be taken to look into their
various properties before any experiments are tried. On
the small place it is possible to make these studies and plant
accordingly.

Where plants are grown particularly for their fruit or
vegetables, and only secondarily for their appearance, of
course they must be given a sunny open spot. Such a garden can often be next the flower garden or lawn if there is
a satisfactory hedge or other screen between them.

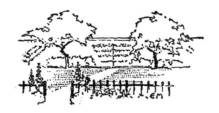

VII

ROCK, WILD, AND WALL GARDENS

Rock gardens are growing in popularity in this country, with good cause. Complete and interesting gardens of this sort need but a small area. They are picturesque, even romantic at times. In them one can get seclusion, even though they are no larger than a living-room indoors.

From the way in which we are working out rock gardens it looks as if they would in time be more peculiarly American than any of our other garden features. In England they are more properly called alpine gardens. There they are designed as suitable places to grow rare "alpines" or mountain flowers, which are often tiny delicate things requiring great care in their upbringing. Such alpine gardens are sunny and open. They are quite unlike any of the native English scenery, though often picturesque.

Much of our American country is rough and ledgy, especially in New England. We see rocky meadows with sparse junipers, cedars, blueberries, and steeplebush all round us. Our woods are filled with exquisite wild flowers and ferns. We love it all, though ignorantly for the most part. When rock gardens are made, we instinctively and correctly try to make something like the ledges we are fond of. While many a choice flowering alpine plant is given a place, yet we treasure the ferns and mosses that come in on the field stone and add to their number. We put in sprawling evergreens as we have seen them in our glorious national park at Mount Desert. In a couple of years the strong native plants begin to crowd out the more delicate imported things. Again and again I have heard the amateur gardener say, "Well, our own ferns are much prettier than the other things. I'm glad to see them spread." In a comparatively short time the rock garden has only a few of the strongest and hardiest of the foreign plants left. Meantime, the gardener has brought in native moss, trillium, hepatica, mayflowers, and other choice wild plants which are given every opportunity to grow. The rock garden that started as an alpine garden has become a wild place of native rock, evergreens, and plants, which are lovelier and more contented than the fussy mountain-plants could ever be.

That is the reason for considering Rock and Wild Gardens together for the Little Garden. It is on the small place that they will be the greatest help and pleasure.

I think of them first as helping to screen the eyesores of the immediate neighborhood. If they are planned when the house is built, then the soil for them will be taken from the cellar hole. A concrete wall four feet or more above the ground where the offending object is most unsightly, — say a garage next door, — tapering off at either end, is first built on the neighbor's boundary lines. Dirt is piled against this wall and stones are laid in to make apparent strata and natural ledges. Pockets and little terraces of soil are left between the stones for plants. Then on top of the bank are put evergreen trees, European beech, a laurel-leaved willow or two for quick effect, or any other dense-foliage tree or shrub. Lower down go cedars, rhododendron, andromeda, and other broad-leaved evergreens. Or, if one is not contented to try them because of the soil, then hawthorns, viburnums, or any favorite native shrubs.

Considerable space is left between these groups of shrubs for smaller plants. In the crannies of the rock go mosses and ferns, spring flowers from the woods, or anything else that will grow and look well. Many alpines will find a place, as well as native plants and even some of the less pointedly garden varieties of bulbs.

Where it is necessary or desirable to narrow the bank, or where a wall is to be built at the outer side of a terrace to hold back the dirt, the sloping, irregular rock-garden may turn imperceptibly into a planted wall. Such a feature is more pleasurable than a meaningless sheet of masonry, and far less expensive to build. When properly made it shows no damage from weather or frost after many years, even where it has the weight of a hillside to retain. The rock garden will be shady if planted with tall trees and shrubs. The wall garden may be partly in the sun, where many plants will grow that would not succeed elsewhere. In spring the wall is covered with flowers. Always it looks green and well if it receives any care whatever. As it is to all intents and purposes a flower bed on end, it increases very much the floweriness of the place. On a small lot this is invaluable.

A double-planted wall makes an excellent separation between lawn and garden or between two gardens. As the principle of separating different parts of the place is most important, the wall is a real help.

There are many books telling how to construct rock gardens, which should be examined before starting any important work. Native ledges and rock-outcrops should be even more carefully studied. In the region of terminal moraines which extends over a considerable territory across the northern part of this country, one will find hills and banks of gravel or soil with rocks here and there projecting above the surface. Such rocks are usually found more or less rounded by prehistoric glacial action. They are impossible to compose in the manner of a ledge. But they can be so built up as to resemble closely the original piling done by the elements, between which soil has been deposited during the succeeding ages. Technically such a construction is usually called a boulder-bank, but it is really one sort of rock garden.

Where there is native rock the problem is not so difficult, especially if it is normally stratified. Stratified rock usually disintegrates in big scales which are parallel at top and bottom but otherwise uneven in shape and size. The student who observes carefully a native ledge of this sort will see that it mounts in almost even walls in some places. In others, it breaks in embryo ravines and irregularities Such walls and accidents can be closely approximated on a small scale in the garden. The natural stratification-lines rarely vary in direction or angle. Consequently, the direction and angle of the artificial ledge must be scrupulously maintained from beginning to end of the work. The care with which this is performed will do more than any other one thing to make the place look natural. Complete success will be met by the visitor's exclamation, "I didn't remember you had a ledge on your place!" As far as possible the stones should have the same color and marking.

Boldness is the great virtue in rock-garden design. Timidity means failure. The effects of miniature precipices, valleys, and slopes must be so exaggerated as to seem like caricatures when building. Piling the rocks on top of each other is tiresome, rather expensive work. But a sheer drop of six or eight feet is none too much to make a good effect.

In any case, the stones should be assembled in ledges and groups, not spread about anywhere as is advised all too often in the books. That makes a " rockery," the abomination of Victorian days, which must be shunned as a gloomy failure.

Behind and between the rocks should be soil well mixed with humus and fertilizer. For most wall-plants, sand is better than clay and peat better than stable manure. Two thirds sandy loam to one third peat makes a good mixture. When building great care must be exercised to get all the holes and crevices soundly filled with soil. Air pockets are anathema to plant-roots. The best procedure is to poke dirt tightly into all the holes with a stout stick and to trample and tamp well all large soil-pockets.

Any precipice of rock is in principle a retaining wall, and must be thick enough to stand indefinitely without bulging or falling down, due to pressure from behind. While soil must fill every crevice, yet every stone must rest at important points on the stone directly underneath it, to keep it solid.

The beginner will be at sea as to the necessary thickness of the wall. At the top it should never be less than twenty inches. At the bottom it must be one third as thick as the total height of the wall measured from the bottom of the foundation to the very top. A wall showing seven feet above the ground on a three-foot foundation must be three and one-half feet wide at the bottom of the foundation. As it goes up it will taper — either outside or in, as may look best.

If the wall be high, at frequent intervals it is well to turn a long stone into the bank where it should rest on other inner and hidden stones. In fact, it is a good thing, if there be a quantity of stone at hand, to build up the core as well as the surface of rock.

Shrubs and trees, even plants, should be put in while the wall is building, since only in that way can their roots be properly spread out and covered with soil. Moreover, they can be thus more prettily fitted into place. Two stones are set up next each other and the plant is laid down between them and its roots covered. Then another stone is placed over the other two, across the roots of the plant. There is no need to be uneasy about laying plants on their sides when planting them. They thrive where so planted in walls.

In this work, too, overplanting is the secret of success. Many varieties will fail at once, and — needless to say — it is impossible to tell, ahead of time, which they will be. In the end the wall must be sufficiently covered with plants in any event. Overplanting is the only way to be sure It is exasperating when a hole is left in one place and the next place is impossibly full of thrifty things that must inevitably begin to kill each other. But that is part of the fortunes of rock-gardening.

Sometimes when planting, especially in a vertical wall, it is impossible to fill the hole over the plant roots, between them and the stone above, because the soil spills out at the front. It is best to have on hand a few pieces of old sod which can be stuffed into the breach, *roots out toward the front*. The grass will die and the sod will hold the dirt behind until it hardens in place.

The stones should be tipped into the wall so that rain will run back to the roots of the plants. At best, the inside of the wall will get very dry.

In a general way these directions apply both to rock gardens and planted walls, which merge one into the other.

VIII

GRADING, STEPS, WALKS

DIFFERENT levels in a garden are always pleasant variations. If terraces and raised borders are foreseen when the house plan is made, then much can be accomplished with the cellar-hole dirt. Emphasis has been put on the desirability of using some of it for a house terrace on the garden side and for a rock garden. Sometimes it may be used quite as effectively in other ways.

A sunken garden always seems to be particularly shut away from the world, though the banks around it are but a foot or so high. There are two ways of making a sunken garden on level ground. One is to scoop out the middle and pile it around the side. This is apt to be expensive. The other is to take soil from elsewhere — the cellar hole again — and put it around the central panel, which is not disturbed. If there is not enough to go around, then a terrace is built across the back opposite the house. The sides can then be made of hedges and shrubs.

If the ground slopes naturally, local conditions and preferences will determine whether it shall be left as it is, or have tucks taken in it in the form of terraces. A natural slope — even across a formal garden — is pleasant if not too marked, provided the planting is loosely rather than stiffly laid out. Such conditions are a challenge to the skilful plantsman, who will reach a balance by using a few taller shrubs or trees on the low side, though not too obvi-

A shady corner terrace in the back yard of a home in an Eastern city. The large trees are all on neighbors' land. This is a comfortable place to gather out of doors.

ously. If the slope does not suit and the soil is easily moved, a horse and slip-scraper can quickly drag some of the dirt from the high side to fill in the low.

Whether sharp slopes be the result of filling or of excavating, their treatment will be about the same. In some parts of the country, enough good-sized stone will be turned up to build little retaining-walls. In other places not a stone will be found and it would be an extravagance to bring it in. Brick walls are costly. Homemade concrete is cheap, especially if done a little at a time. Low walls will not require any reënforcement of iron rods, though all concrete is the better for it. The United States Agricultural Department has useful pamphlets on homemade concrete construction.[1] The more rough and irregular the finished surface, the better. The holes fill with dirt and moss while vines cling at once to a rough wall to which no waterproofing has been applied.

Sharp slopes, such as one often sees, are commonly covered with grass, which does poorly. A grass-covered slope is excessively dry. It is scarred by the gouging toes of anyone who has tried to find a foothold on it. The grass is aggravating to cut; it takes more time for maintenance than it deserves. There are other ways of covering a slope more satisfactorily. Ground-cover plants will enjoy it. And bushes will hold it firm with matted roots.

Steps will be needed to get from level to level. They need not be expensive. The simplest are made by laying posts along the bank, holding them in place by driving in stout

[1] Farmers' Bulletins Nos. 481 and 1279 give valuable information about homemade concrete structures, including walls, pools, and so on. They can be procured from the Superintendent of Documents, Washington, D. C.

pegs toward either end, cut off flush with the top. They will look better if mortised into the posts. These prone timbers become the risers of the steps. The treads are of gravel, which is filled in behind each riser. Or the treads can be made with turf, which will need a good deal of watering in dry weather. These steps will be easier to use and look somewhat more shipshape if the posts are split and the flat side turned toward the front.

In other cases the risers can be made of stone or concrete bars, filled in behind. And in other cases the tread can be filled in with a paving of brick or stone, which can be laid dry in sand or cinders if the riser be firm and strong.

Where stone is cheap, stone steps are easy to build, either with or without mortar. Except in much " slicked up " places, it is prettier to lay them dry, so that plants will grow between them. What matter if they get heaved a bit during the winter? An hour in the spring with a crowbar and shovel will set them sufficiently to rights. And this will seldom be necessary, as dry-laid stone steps are well drained by the nature of their construction.

IX

GARDEN–FURNISHING

GARDEN-FURNISHING, like house-furnishing, serves two purposes. Practically, it is to make the place comfortable to live in and easy to maintain. Otherwise, it is for appearance' sake. Common sense calls for comfort first and mere decoration afterwards.

Unfortunately, many garden-makers think only of appearance, and this tendency has been exploited by dealers, who show ten Renaissance marble seats to one sensible wooden bench. Stone or concrete is uncomfortable to sit on for any length of time. Furthermore, there is an antithesis in the decorative versus the livable location of furniture. To be decorative, in any large sense, it must be seen. To be livable, it must be secluded. A marble seat at the end of a garden in full view of the house is precisely the place where one would not go to spend a quiet afternoon.

The first duty of a garden-designer is to plan agreeable "sitting-rooms" out under shady trees and in screened corners. Each one will be fitted to its probable use. For games or tea, there will be benches and seats for four or five people at least, and a table. In the table drawer, or a box tacked on to a bench somewhere, should be a stiff clothes-scrubbing brush and a good-sized rag with which the dirt that gathers on everything can be cleaned off. At least a ten-foot square should be allowed for such a group. If it is not altogether in the shade, the designer will figure in advance at what time of day it will be most used and locate it accordingly.

It will be difficult to keep grass in good condition under such a place. Other material would make a better floor. Flagstone or brick, laid on a foot of cinders and a bed of sand, will serve the purpose. The materials can often be bought cheaply from house-wrecking establishments or when old sidewalks are being replaced. Rough country stone is attractive, but in most parts of the country has so ragged a surface that tables and chairs can never find a firm foothold on it.

Where stone or brick is not available, a packed gravel surface will do equally well. A gravel platform should have a definite edge of brick or stone set on end. Otherwise there will be a permanently messy line where it meets turf or beds. The edging can be plunged down almost out of sight and little plants encouraged to grow over it. But it should be there, marking a definite line to sweep to on one side and to plant against on the other.

Quantities of cigarette and cigar stubs thrown about will soon make any garden shabby. Little ash-trays are a nuisance out of doors. A big concrete oil-jar will make a capital trash-holder and be decorative at the same time. Big jars will be useful everywhere for trash, weeds, faded flowers, and the endless débris that must be constantly cleaned away. They should be put where most convenient, like waste-paper baskets indoors. In nine cases out of ten such a place will be the best for appearance as well. Except in an extremely formal garden, such objects should have a touch of the casual, or they will make the place stiff and unhomelike.

It is a mistake to put a bird bath near the gathering

place of many people. It should be more isolated, with a single bench near by, perhaps, for the interested person who can keep still. Bird baths require a word of warning. In all reason they should be installed for the good of the birds, not as a trap to bring them to the very jaws of the family cat. If birds avoid a shallow clean pool on the ground or surrounded by bushes the blame may fairly be thrown on cats, whether or not they are ever seen on the premises. Most people fail to keep an eye on the bird bath at five o'clock in the morning.

Where there are cats, a bird bath should be put in the open, on a cat-proof pedestal well off the ground. Where cats can be kept absolutely out — as they should be by every one who has the slightest interest in birds — a bird bath may be put almost anywhere, though birds apparently prefer to have a bit of sun. Experts say that they like to have a bush near by on which to perch and shake, or else that they detest such a location, with other bits of conflicting advice. After building various sorts of fountains and waterways, above and on the ground, in sun and in woodland, for other purposes altogether, I have found that birds like to bathe in most unexpected and unlikely places. Apparently they are satisfied in almost any place where they can find a firm foothold and shallow water either quiet or gently moving. When they are securely at home they resent the intrusion of any outsider. A visiting human being or dog, especially if noisy, is greeted from every branch by a chorus of twittering expostulation, often lasting until the stranger is driven out by his own evil conscience.

The most appropriate and the prettiest bird-baths are not formal basins or carved fountains, but the little pools and runways of a rock garden. There the birds are most at home and are charming to see fluttering over the stones and dipping into the water — not in one place, but here and there as fancy dictates.

Pools and running water are a part of the garden's poetry. Important waterworks, like all plumbing, are costly and outside the Little Garden problem for the most part. But that need not deter the average gardener from introducing water for pleasure. At its simplest, a tar barrel cut in halves and filled with a hose will suffice for a water lily. Concrete is not difficult to manage, as many a homemade pool goes to prove in gardens and farmyards all over the country.[1] In fact, the concrete or masonry is the simplest part of the problem. The difficulty lies in managing Jack Frost. He has a way of crawling under steps, wall, or pool and heaving the freezing earth till they look in spring as if tumbled and cracked by an earthquake. The trouble does not come about in the things themselves, but in the foundations under the things. If all water can be kept out of the foundations down to a point below frost-action, all will go well. For it is the expansion of freezing water in an already full volume that raises hob.

Consequently, adequate foundations have to be either solid down to the frost line, or else they must be porous so that any water getting into them is immediately drained away. That is why cinders and sand will serve the purpose. The depth to which the foundation must be built will differ from place to place according to the severity of winter. In Maine frost is found five or six feet below the surface; in Philadelphia, rarely more than eighteen inches.

A shallow pool is most effective to bring out the crystal

1 See footnote, page 61.

A black mirror pool in a sunken garden. The terrace is retained by a dry planted wall. The hedge is made on the garden side of the taller boundary-planting. This could all be easily put in the back yard of a lot 75 by 150 feet.

quality and color of clear water. Such pools are fitly painted light blue and green. But these colors are a mistake where the water is turbid and brown, for it then looks dirty always and the pool looks muddy. Deep pools are rarely made to bring out the clarity of the water itself, but rather for the reflecting quality of their surface. Narcissus must have gazed in a deep dark pool, for none other would have pleased him with his own reflection. Sky, flowers, foliage, light and shadow seem more brilliant when reflected from a black quiet pool than when seen directly. There is a trick by which pools can be made to seem much deeper and darker than they are, namely, painting the bottom black, blue-black, or brown-black, whichever gives the best effect. This will depend on the color of the water itself, and only experiment can prove which should be used. The illusion of depth fails on a pool that is less than two feet deep, ordinarily. But even so, the effect of a mirror surface is not lost in the shallowest black pools, if the bottom can be kept clean.

Because of the chemical action of salts which work out to the surface of concrete, paints often fail to make a good bond and flake off after a time. Furthermore, ordinary paints are mixed with linseed oil. This combines with the lime in the concrete mixture to form a soapy, scummy surface, which looks dirty and in time disintegrates. Shallow pools, however, are apt to be prettier when the painted surface is not too mechanically even in tone, so that the appearance may be actually improved if the paint chips off, leaving the white surface showing through. To avoid excessive evenness and artificiality of tone, a mixture of blue and white, modulating much in the fashion of thin white clouds against blue sky, is particularly pretty.

Unless there is a constant flow of water, the garden pool will be an ideal breeding-ground for mosquitoes. This can be corrected by putting in half a dozen goldfish, which thrive on the mosquito larvæ and grow fat. They should not be fed with other things, but made to attend strictly to business for all their nourishment.

Fountains are a sparkling pleasure when running. Too often they are depressing, even ugly, when without the spouting water that is necessary to complete their design. Besides, there is a neglected and useless look about most fountains that do not run, as if a place were being left without care. On the other hand, as long as the fountains play, no amount of neglect can deprive the garden of its power to please, as many a place in Italy goes to prove.

An inexhaustible supply of running water is built into such Italian gardens, where it is cheaper to let them run than to buy the machinery to turn them off. That is rarely the case in this country. Instead, here water is paid for by the gallon, and the slightest tendency to make free with it in summer is usually summarily checked by authorities whose eyes are on the surface of sinking reservoirs. Consequently, it is worth while getting fountains — especially on small places where they are always conspicuous — which look well as decoration when the water does not play. Few of the stock patterns are suitable in this respect, especially for important locations in the centres of gardens. It is better in most cases to put them at the far end of a place. There, with the backing of a bit of wall or a niche and a bench, with delicate vines draping over them, with flowers and bushes roundabout, perhaps under the shadow of tall trees, their peculiar function as fountains is less obvious and their purpose as interesting features to focus attention upon in the distance is emphasized. An isolated position is hard on any object save one of great beauty, exactly fitted to its conspicuous place.

In connection with axes, it was noted that one of their functions is to indicate that there is a definite end of the garden where one may stop, satisfied. An insignificant feature should not be used for the purpose, naturally. A flowerpot, whether small or large, is, when all is said, insignificant. It should not be forced to play the sole part of terminating the axis, though it may be put on the line as an item of decoration in a more important composition. That is the reason why urns and vases against a green background are misplaced at the end of an axis, where they are commonly seen. It is necessary to put a wall behind them, or columns, or some other feature larger and more important than they are themselves.

In fact, the composition of objects in groups is too little understood. Once started, there is a temptation to get too many things and then sprinkle them about with the idea of " making the most of them." The attention is scattered. The decoration is thin and spotty. A fountain, a couple of seats, and jars should be composed as one group at some important spot which will command attention. This will do more to furnish a garden than any number of unrelated things here and there.

Garden furniture must have a good background. A bench out on the open lawn is forlorn. If the object deserves to be brought out, it should be placed against a contrasting color and material: if white, against a dark green hedge; if bronze-green, against a white niche or the sky. If the design requires its subordination, the same color or value should be used as a background. This is especially true of wooden benches and tables. They should look comfortable, nothing more. They are best when the natural wood is oiled and they weather the color of tree trunks and arbor poles   If they must be painted, then neutral gray-green or greenish-blue — more rarely, dull dark red or plum-color — should be the colors, never white. Staring white benches against the green are inhospitable from a distance and always dirty.

The same suggestions apply to arbors and trellises, in fact to all wooden objects save fences and palings. White-colored seats, grape-arbors, and pergolas are in effect hardest to cover with vines. They stand out from the garden instead of falling into place. Sometimes, if the house is white with green blinds, it is possible to combine the two colors in the other structures. The proportions should be the reverse of those used on the house; a little white and much green will look better.

X

SERVICE–FEATURES, ARBORS, FENCES

THERE is a good deal of machinery about life in the simplest home and, if the gardener is to have any time to attend to his or her special work, the ordinary burdens must be lightened as much as civilization can do it. When discussing service-areas incident to the kitchen, it is the women who are directly concerned. Nowadays, it looks as if the ladies needed no masculine help in getting over curbstones and into automobiles, as they once did. Chivalry turns to other channels, and one of them is in the direction of helping to make life a little more easy and pleasant for the woman who does her own housework. Indoors there are numberless contrivances toward this end. Out of doors there are fewer and even those have received comparatively little attention.

It was the ease with which the colonial housewife could step back and forth from kitchen to arbor and yard that made of these outdoor places cool extensions of her hot kitchen. The same scheme should be worked out to-day. If the housework is to be done by the owner, then it is best to have the kitchen windows open wide and deep on the garden side. What could be more agreeable than a breakfast alcove looking out to a fresh, orderly garden of a summer's morning? If the kitchen door gives on to the house terrace, so much the better. The bench and tables used occasionally for tea or lemonade will do as well for shelling peas.

Convenient way from laundry to drying-yard is necessary where any household washing is done at home. Modern stationary tubs are sometimes put in the kitchen, sometimes in a separate room. In either case, heavy baskets of wet laundry must be carried out to the line to dry. Under the best of conditions this is a heavy burden for a woman. It must not be made worse by having dark crooked hallways, flights of steps, or long walks, between tub and line. Any decent, foresighted designer will see to that.

The laundry yard must be close to the house. It must be dry and clean both winter and summer. Lines must be easily put up and taken down. They must be far enough from walls and fences so that waving clothes can't flap in the wind against the dirty surfaces. They must be high enough from the ground to allow for hanging sheets. Six feet seems to suit the average needs. The distance between two lines should be at least twenty inches. The maximum length of line will be determined in each case by the size of the wash.

An area fifteen by twenty feet should be more than enough for the laundry yard of a small house.

When possible, the clothes should have the full benefit of sun and breeze. They must not be overhung by the branches of trees or any other thing from which dirty water could be expected to drip.

Following the rule for the frank separation of areas, the laundry yard will be divided from lawn and garden by arbor, trellis, or planting. The height and density of the screen will depend largely on personal preference. There is nothing particularly objectionable in theory in the sight of clean clothes hanging in the sun. But some people are at ease only when the work of life is out of sight and mind.

They will want a high close screen between them and it. Others will enjoy the sight of a chore well done.

The old arbors were usually made of cedar, chestnut, or locust posts, cleaned of their bark, set in lines from six to eight feet apart and from seven to nine feet high. White cedar or spruce poles were tacked on from post to post, ladder-like, on which grape vines were trained. Across the top was a mesh of similar poles. This still makes the best arbor of a fairly rustic sort. The large posts will last a long time if their bark is removed so that insects can get no hidden foothold from which to bore their way into the wood. If they are charred or well soaked with creosote below the ground, — into which they must be firmly set from three to four feet, — their usefulness will be much prolonged. The light poles can be replaced without much bother when they rot.

Where a little more elegance is fitting, the posts are the same, but planed-wood strips two to three inches wide and one to one and a half inches thick are used instead of the light poles. The top can be arched and the ends decorated with trellis work.

A slightly more imposing structure can be made with simple round or square cement posts, which will not look well if less than ten inches in diameter. Stone, planed or carved wood-columns, masonry piers, and so on, are a good deal used for more pretentious structures of the sort. In such cases the strips up the side are usually omitted and the vines trained to grow up the posts to reach the top. Then they become pergolas rather than arbors.

The pergola is an Italian feature more or less adapted to this country. Americans have too often tried to refine their European prototypes — with stupid results. The original pergolas are built on all sorts of posts, even elaborately carved marble. But the roof of poles remains, easy to renew and gratefully gripped by the tendrils of the vine. These irregular poles cover quickly with a mantle of leaves and even when bare, cast picturesque, thin checkered shadow. Our architects are not satisfied with that. They make a roof of heavy planed boards with carved ends, like the unceiled framework of a house room. This unnecessarily heavy structure is then painted uncompromisingly white. Vines do not like such things, so they stay naked for years. Meantime, they cast hard bars of shade lacking any charm. They are ostentatious without luxury. Nothing could be worse. No matter how elaborate the pergola posts, the covering framework should be of simple poles.

Summerhouses are built in much the same way, but they are shaped like rooms rather than long corridors. The chief difference lies in their having a solid roof of any material that design or pocketbook requires. One or more of their walls may be solid, pierced with doors or windows. They may have a floor of wood, stone, tile, or brick. They are suitable subjects for elaboration.

The simplest trellis is like one side of an arbor standing alone. On this framework, fancy has played many variations. The strips are crossed and put close together in squares, diamond shapes, and circles. Their outlines are elaborated in rococo shapes. Fancy openings are cut in their plain or paneled surfaces. Urns and finials accent their silhouettes. They are so easily adapted to fanciful design that the original material and use — that of a vine-support — is forgotten, and they are handled almost like so much decorative cloth, hung on walls, on the insides of buildings as well as out. They never lose their outdoor

Plan and photograph by Bremer W. Pond, Landscape Architect.

A summerhouse connected with a simple arbor — appropriate to the small American-type house.

association, however, which makes them suitable for sun-rooms and outdoor living-rooms.

Fences are in a sense much like trellises. Everybody knows what fences are good for, though few people use them enough nowadays. Even a low paling, over which one can see unobstructed, secludes and marks off an area to an extent surprising when one stops to think how insignificant it really is. In the old days every American home was set within a white fence — a sensible custom. Nowadays, when wandering bands of heedless boys and girls sweep through the streets, leaving broken bushes and ruined grass-edges in their wake, a low fence is often just enough to protect a place. In olden times a good fence was " bull-proof, hog-tight, and horse-high," not a bad rule, though nowadays we should say, " man-proof." Such fences are now made of coarse wire mesh, hung on an iron framework. They are almost invisible and really imperative where fruit and vege-tables, not to speak of flowers, need protection. Few of the cheaper farm-fences will keep boys out. High pickets set close together or solid board fences are rather a chal-lenge to a lively youngster, who manages somehow to pry off a picket and get through. Besides, they don't last very long and are expensive to build and repair. The woven wire is not cheap, but it is the best.

Not only the laundry yard but the garage drive is now a necessity of the small place. Garage drives are many-fashioned. Wheel tracks are enough for the mechanical operation. When they are flush with the ground, twenty inches is wide enough to stay on easily when going forward. Backing is a different matter. A sunken track is easier to manœuvre in, but it is hard on tires when square and deep. A shallow, gutter-like depression with sloping sides is more

economical. But the depression must be marked enough
to enable the machine almost to find its own way. And the
tires on both sides must be exactly in the bottom of the
tracks. The width between wheels differs, with a large dis-
crepancy between small cars and trucks. Trolley tracks
are spaced four feet eight inches apart. One can judge
from that.

Tracks should have their edges clearly marked, unless a
straggly edge in the manner of old farm-lanes is neat
enough. Small cobblestones, — or, as they are variously
known, kidney or popple stones, — laid on end lengthwise
with the drive, make good tracks. They are dark or soon
discolor in the weather. Their lines are blurred somewhat,
which is more sightly than stiff white concrete strips.

In some situations it will look better to have a drive the
full width, which is easier to back on without running over
the edges. Such a drive should be at least eight feet wide.
Hedges and shrubs must not be permitted to overhang the
drive, so their future growth must be discounted when
planting alongside.

Small places can't waste room on an ordinary full turn-
around for cars. Yet at times a way to change direction
near the garage is a help. The up-to-date solution is called
a Y-turn. A quarter-circle drive is built off the straight
drive, the centre line being on a radius of at least twenty-
nine feet — more is better for a large car. The end of the
quarter-circle is extended to allow the car to back in far
enough to be straight in its tracks, or almost so. Then
it can go forward in the opposite direction from which it
started. A Y-turn uses but little room, comparatively.
At times, when used rather as an emergency than a regular
thing, the Y end can also be used as a clothes-drying yard.

When ice and snow are not too troublesome and its use can be dispensed with in winter, an iron turntable in the drive takes up no room and is easy to manage. During freezing weather it is apt to be stuck tight where ice fills the cracks around the edge.

On rather light soils with good drainage, both surface and underground, grass will stand much harder use than is ordinarily supposed. It has been proved at many country houses that heavy automobiles can come over the lawn to the door a dozen times a day leaving hardly more than a temporary track. It is necessary to have a very hard firm turf on a well-packed foundation, of course. And for a month or two in spring it is in peril, at that. At other times it may serve very well.

Where the gardener wants such a turf-drive on a heavier soil, special preparation is required. The tracks are given a Telford-stone foundation. This means that stones six to ten inches across are carefully fitted together on end with a fairly level top. Any holes between are then filled with crushed trap-rock, with a light finish of peatstone to prevent their clogging up. Then three to four inches of sandy loam are packed down next, and finally all is sodded. The tracks are thus well drained and firm and the grass roots can push out on either side to get the benefit of deeper soil. In a country where rocks abound, this is not an elaborate operation, though it may sound so. One laborer, properly bossed, can accomplish wonders with dirt and stone on a small place. Needless to say, such a grass pavement requires plenty of sun and water.

XI

TOOLHOUSE AND COLD FRAMES

No feature of a garden is more important than the tool-house. In fact, it is safest for every gardener to begin with a place where all the necessary tools can be kept neatly and in good order. For some reason a woman who is fastidious about the arrangement and order of the dining-room and kitchen pantry is willing to have an old dark corner where garden tools are thrown almost pell-mell. It is a great extravagance not to keep tools in good condition, as they become useless in no time if allowed to stay rusty and dirty. A list of necessary tools should be made up very carefully and a place arranged for each and every one of them. At the end of the day the gardener should invariably look over the toolhouse to see that everything is in its place and in good condition. This is easy to do where things are in order, and very difficult otherwise. The toolhouse should include not only the necessary tools, but also pockets for plant-stakes and labels, for various commercial fertilizers, for Bordeaux mixture, kerosene emulsion, and other things. Without the right tools gardening-maintenance is a wearisome thing. With the right tools it may be one of the truest interests of life. The tools cannot be kept in good condition or easily available unless there is a proper place for them.

The plate shows a toolhouse which is much simpler than it looks at first. It is nothing more than some shelves and hooks fastened to a high board-fence. It is protected on the top by a sloping board-roof covered with tar paper, and on the open side by a screen of cheap, ready-made doors.

A high fence is useful as a screen somewhere, even on the smallest place. The toolhouse may start with only one compartment and be added to from time to time as the need grows. Most people would be able to get along at first with only half the area shown. No two gardeners would agree on the things that are indispensable. The following is a long but not excessive list to suit average needs:—

Hoe	Grub hoe
Scuffle hoe	Crowbar
D-handle shovel (round)	Two pails
Spade	Pruning saw
Manure fork	Soil-sieve
Digging fork	Sickle
Edging knife	Garden line
Edge-clippers (long	Bin for commercial ferti-
sheep-shears)	lizer
Wheelbarrow	Bin for lime
Large watering can	Bin for humus
Long-necked watering can	Bin for propagating-
Lawn-mower	sand
Oil-can	Shelf-flats for seeds
Funnel	4′ plant-stakes
Wrench	2′ and 3′ plant-stakes
100 ft. garden hose	Large wood garden-stakes
Sprinkler	10″ garden labels
4-bushel basket	Pot-labels
Two market-baskets	Twine and raffia
Barn broom	Shelf for pots
Planet Jr. seeder	Small sprayers with hose
Iron rake	and nozzles
Wooden rake	Hand-sprayer for powder
Pick	Insecticides

Pruning shears (long-handled hedge)

Pruning shears (long-handled clippers)

Hand pruning-shears (for shrubs)

Small hand pruning-shears for flowers

Scissors

Trowels

Dibble

Hand cultivator

Ladder (hung on outside)

There are a few extras that will be a comfort as time goes on. A seat built in where one can do little tinkering jobs and collect one's thoughts when alone is one of them. A hook over it will be useful for the " help " that come in for occasional heavy work. The seat is a good place for the man to have his lunch. An extra compartment for the unexpected will be almost a necessity. No one ever foresees all the things that gradually accumulate. Moreover, if all the trash is gathered in one place, the rest can more simply be kept neat.

Half a dozen things may be bought at one time. Then the others can be added as the tyro becomes expert and sees the need.

More money can be saved on a small place with cold frames and hotbeds than in any other way. With them almost all herbaceous and annual plants can be started from seeds ; shrubs and trees from cuttings.

The best place for them is on the south side of a building or hedge, where the sun shines all day and cold winds are kept off. The standard size of glass sash is three feet by six feet, so the frames are made six feet long and a multiple of three feet wide. The front should be just above the ground level, to keep out water. The back is made six inches higher than the front, to shed water. The front is always toward the sun, to catch the early slanting rays.

While they may be made of plank, concrete retains the heat better and is more durable. Homemade concrete walls six inches thick will do. The foundation should go below frost. As it is difficult to make concrete smooth enough on top to fit tightly against the sash, it is better to set the heads of bolts into the concrete when making. Afterwards a two-inch by four-inch piece of cypress can be bolted on and planed to fit the sash. It will pay to paint all the woodwork, as it lasts longer and prevents the boards from checking and warping.

Hotbeds are made the same way. Inside there must be room for from one to three feet of fresh stable-manure under four inches of soil, plus room for the plants to grow.

The manure for hotbeds must be fresh and should contain a fair amount of straw or coarse material. If wood chips were used for bedding, either straw or leaves should be mixed with the manure in equal bulk, to make a gentle lasting heat instead of one which is intense and quickly disappears.

After turning the manure-pile on three successive days, it is ready to go into the hotbed. Put it in in layers a foot deep, tramping each one down firmly, — not too firmly, — and then wet it. If flats are to be used for growing the plants, spread a two-inch layer of soil over the manure, put on the sash, and wait for the first intense heat to pass away. The frame is ready for seeds when the temperature has dropped to 80°. This takes from five to fifteen days.

Soil in which seeds are to be planted directly should be sandy loam mixed with one third leaf-mould, four inches to five inches deep, on top of the manure.

A temporary hotbed which is much easier and pleasanter to use — because of its height — may be made as follows:

Stake out a rectangle on the ground which shall be three feet wider and three feet longer than the hotbed. Build within this a pile of manure three feet high, a foot at a time, and thoroughly tamp each layer. On this pile place the hotbed frame, made with a front twelve inches high and a back eighteen inches. Pack in manure around it up to the top on all sides. The loam is then placed inside as in a permanent frame.

In any case surface water must be carefully drained away, as it will make the manure so wet it will not heat.

XII

EXAMPLES

THE conditions of every problem in design are different. Lots vary in size, exposure, and topography. Trees are scattered about. Houses are not the same. No two people want just the same thing. That is the reason why the expert hesitates when asked to precipitate details in a flood of generalities. There is too much machine-made " art " in the world, as it is.

It is helpful to the uninitiated to be given " examples," nevertheless, to show him how principles are applied to special cases. At least, they make his mind more supple when he turns to his own.

Suppose Mr. and Mrs. Brown to be intelligent young people who want a home with a bit of land about it. They have found a neighborhood where they like the people. Streets, water, light, and so forth are satisfactory. The lots average 75 feet on the street and 125 in depth. They have found three possible lots for sale at the same price, all on the south side of a street running east and west. On all of them are houses with identical setback from the street and floor area (no unusual thing), and a one-car garage. In all the back yards are five good trees that — by a miracle confined to writers — are relatively in precisely the same places. Which shall they buy?

They looked first at No. 15 because it was so " attractive." It stood back from the street in a neat yard. It

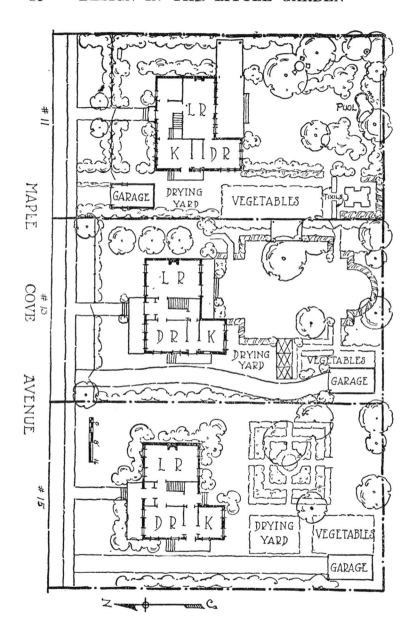

had a front verandah and " planting around the foundations," which they had seen recommended in nursery cata-
logues.   The garage was out of the way in a far corner.
They liked the house with its nice hall, large living-room
on the east, and dining-room on the west, behind which were
kitchen and pantries.   Mrs. Brown was delighted to find
a formal garden set down in the back yard.   The hedges
and flowers looked a bit ragged, for which they blamed a
couple of the trees.   They thought that two of them would
have to be cut down, which seemed a pity, as they hid the
houses on the next street.   There was also a bed of vegetables and a laundry yard.   Mrs. Brown made up her mind
that they were lucky to find such a place.   As they sat a
moment on the front verandah, she started to tell her husband that it seemed a waste of time to go further, but was
interrupted by a passing truck, which made a racket and
left behind a trail of blue smoke.   She sighed and remarked
that it was impossible to get away from the city, no matter
where one went.

They made their way to No. 13, which looked much the
same, garage and all, save that it had a fence and planting
across the front.   Mrs. Brown instantly said that she would
never live in a house without a front verandah, even. if
automobiles did roar and smoke.   But to please her husband
she went in and found the house like the other, so there was
no complaint on that score.

When she came to the south French window of the living
room, she called out, " My dear, look at this.   There's
some mistake.   It's a bigger lot "; for so it looked.   Just
outside the window was a narrow corridor-like terrace, with
steps down through gay flower-beds to a considerable lawn
with hedges around it.   On walking out they found at the

left a cozy screened-in structure, much larger than the usual garden-house, with a big table and comfortable chairs. "Henry!" she exclaimed, "I want to give a bridge party here next week." Henry never lost his amazement at his wife's ability to haul the indefinite future into the immediate present. He still wanted to look about. And she began to point out further charms.

"It's so cool here. I love the way you look across the sun-and-shadow lawn through that covered, dark grape-arbor across the way. That leads to the garage. And see the rose path out here in the sun. What a lot of flowers for so small a place! Henry! If that's not a little bird-fountain at the end of the lawn in that alcove!"

Next the garage they found a bit of a vegetable garden and some cold frames. At the kitchen corner was a laundry yard of clean gravel, from which Mr. Brown said it would be easy to shovel snow in winter. Grass in winter thaws is apt to get muddy. Moreover, he thought it might be easily fixed so that his wife could back the machine into it and turn around. She hated backing a long way. One was so apt to run into things. The more they looked the place over the better they liked it. Mrs. Brown was now quite convinced that it was wasting time to look further, especially as No. 11 was unprepossessing from the street.

"What on earth do you suppose made them put the garage on the street? And there is no front yard! It looks queer to me." Henry said it made him curious to know what was inside. He liked the hawthorn bushes by the front walk and had always wanted to live behind a gate, "away from things."

Once inside, Mrs. Brown admitted that it was nice to be fenced away from the street, which was now quite out of sight. She liked the fern beds and Solomon's seal by the front porch, too.

She wondered why they put plants all over the ground. They were like garden beds. Henry expected to handle the lawn mower and thought it might be a good thing to reduce the grass area. Besides, the grass on the north side of the other houses hadn't amounted to much.

When they discovered that the kitchen was on the street side they both felt that the fitness of things had been absurdly and needlessly affronted. "It's insulting to guests to put it next the front door — though, to be sure, we never guessed it from the outside. That's because of the range of high windows toward the street." The hall was tiny, but, to make up for it, there was a small reception room at the left.

The living-room was flooded with sunlight from windows all across the south side. It was far pleasanter than those of the other houses, though the same size. Outside was a terrace, " just like a country house."

"Henry! we could *eat* out there Sunday nights, looking on that delicious little wild corner. Do you suppose they found a lovely spot like that in this commonplace neighborhood? My dear, that's a pool beyond the bushes, and rocks and rhododendrons and flowers in the crannies. This is too good to be true! "

They found a rose bed with four standard roses in the four corners, which explained why the garage had to go elsewhere. Next was a vegetable garden which seemed actually large. The laundry yard was next the house.

"After all," said Mrs. Brown, " there really wasn't any other place for the garage, was there? Just see what a lot of room the other places waste with their drives."

When they thought they had been all over the place, they went again to the terrace to sit a moment in the screened-in room across from the dining-room. " Well, if that isn't almost too much," cried Mrs. Brown on looking around. For, alongside the house, enclosed by clipped hedges with a bench at the further end, was an almost hidden garden of iris in full bloom.

" Why — do you see? That bench in the hedge is where the front yard ought to be! Who would have thought it could be hidden away right next to the sidewalk? "

The cost of building and planting 11, 13, and 15 Maple Cove Avenue would be the same. Dollar for dollar and foot for foot, there is little question which one is the best for the money or gets the most out of the land.

XIII

DETAILS OF NO. 13 MAPLE COVE AVENUE

FORMAL GARDEN

THE BROWNS found three finished places. Their good judgment showed them in a general way the good and bad qualities of the designs. Many of the details escaped them at first. Let us hope that they learned to know in good time the little things which may make the execution of any plan either good or bad.

The setback of the house from the street is often one of the fixed restrictions put on suburban land when it is sold, and it has been assumed here to be thirty feet. A good deal more is often required, — quite needlessly, — the excuse being that the whole street looks better when the houses are pushed well back. The fact is, of course, that it is the way the fronts of the lots look — not their size — that makes the streets handsome or ugly. In this country we like generous spaces, and where new land is laid out it may be well to reserve an open strip ten or fifteen feet wide between sidewalk and any structures. But the burden of decorating and maintaining that strip, which is frankly devoted to the general welfare, should be distributed generally. Within the boundaries of his own property a man should be allowed to do as he pleases, with due regard for his neighbors in the avoidance of nuisances of smell, sight, hearing, or sanitation. Any restriction that requires the owner to keep the view open from the highway over any part of his land is both impertinent and obnoxious. Yet one of the common land-restrictions forbids putting up any fence or hedge whatever on the street line, or higher than three feet at any place nearer the sidewalk than the setback distance of the house. There would be as little sense in requiring that all houses have windows open to the floor, which should never be covered to prevent the passer-by from looking in. The sensible procedure is to put attractive but high impenetrable fences and hedges along the street. Then windows and doors can be kept wide open in hot weather without the annoyance of exposure to the public eye.

A high board-fence is, truly, rather an ugly thing. But a high colonial picket-fence is a particularly attractive feature of some old streets. And within it a hedge of lilac or arborvitæ makes an opaque yet not forbidding barrier. It cuts off not only vision, but street noise, smells, and dirt, which are increasing by rapid stages of torment.

A good fence may cost more than one can afford. In that case a hedge alone may serve. But hedges will not always keep out children, dogs, and cats. Then the hedge can be reënforced by putting a strong wire fence between two rows of planting. Most hedges are stronger and better for being planted in double rows. The plants soon cover the fence and the wires give a useful added protection. If the gardener intends to use fruit trees in the front yard, he will need protection.

In regions where the land rises steeply from the street, we are getting accustomed to seeing garages sensibly put on the sidewalk. The practical reason is obvious to all. It would often be impossible to get into them with an automobile, otherwise. The drive would be too steep. If the

garage alone had to be considered, a place could be found
for it in the rear of most lots, provided there was a real
objection to it elsewhere. The garage is a small part of
the difficulty. The drive into it takes the room. On many
small places a good quarter of the total lot-area is devoted
to garage and drive. Then gardens, rose beds, vegetables,
all have to be sacrificed to the drive on land which they
might otherwise occupy. It is a mistake. Garages can be
made neat and attractive. They belong near the street
where they will take up the minimum space.

There is still in some places a regulation against putting
garages under or adjoining a residence. They should be
fireproof under such circumstances, by all means. Otherwise it is an excellent way to get rid of them, reducing the
cost of building and the area to be covered. The success
of this solution where it has been tried can be definitely
proven.

Another restriction which sometimes interferes with a
sensible arrangement forbids putting the house or any part
of it within ten or fifteen feet of either side of the lot. This
is reasonable to protect everybody's light and air on wide
lots. But it is a mistake on a narrow lot. One gets better results by having almost no room on one side and a comparatively wide area on the other, rather than a narrow
dark corridor on both. The narrow corridor can never
support plant life. A wider strip may be transformed into
a garden, even if most of it be paved and walled. Where
there is neither light, air, nor soil it is unfair to expect
anything to grow. Yet the ailanthus tree seems to flourish
in the hearts of cities where conditions for plant life are
gloomy and forbidding. Virginia creeper (*Ampelopsis
engelmanni*) and wistaria climb out through pavements to

cover dirt-stained walls. The persistency and courage of plant life are amazing.

Whether the plan be formal or informal, the underlying principle decrees that the beauty of the garden lies in its arrangement, not in the varieties of plants with which it is decorated. Plants, shrubs, and trees in the garden are but the materials with which it is built. Stone, brick, wood-plank, gravel, water are others. Sky is still another, and the least intelligently used of all.

The only safe way to design a formal garden is with pencil and paper. At any store furnishing architects' supplies one can get paper by the yard divided into inch squares. These squares in turn are subdivided into eight parts, each little square being $\frac{1}{8}''$ on a side. Architects' house plans are usually drawn on a scale of which one inch on paper represents four feet of the finished structure. When the special paper is used, the same scale is easy to manage. An inch on the paper equals four feet on the ground. One-eighth of an inch equals one-half a foot or six inches. A map of a lot 75 feet wide and 125 feet long can thus be drawn to scale on a paper approximately 19 x 32 inches.

First, the outline of the whole lot should be drawn. Then the house plan should be accurately located. When the plan is made before the house is built, it is a good idea to draw the house plan on stiff paper. It can then be cut out and moved about as one works over the garden plan, until exactly the right place for the future house is determined. It is quite likely that the site decided upon after study of the garden plan will be several feet in one direction or another away from where it would have been " naturally " but blindly located without the future garden-plan.

This little change may make all the difference between a good and a bad garden.

When finally fixed, the floor plan is put in the correct relative position on the paper plan. When the house is already built, its exact location is determined by measuring to the corners from the known boundaries. The locations of rooms, windows, doors, and verandahs are next shown. Generally they can be traced directly from the architect's blueprint.

After that, one locates other things by measuring from various corners, known objects, and places, getting every point from at least two other already known points. For instance, to locate a tree one measures two straight lines to it from two corners of the lot or from one corner of the lot and one of the house — supposing the latter to be already drawn on the plan. In this way one shows the place of all buildings, trees, rocks, shrubs, and any other objects of the slightest importance. When done, this is really a map of the conditions which must be coped with.

Our formal scheme is balanced symmetrically on the axis of a living-room window. It is assumed that house and garage were already in place. The width of the open grass-panel in the middle is determined by the distance between this axis and the east side of the lot. Along the boundary a heavy shrub-planting is needed to shut out the next place and to make an agreeable enclosure of the lawn itself. The minimum width for such a planting is 9 feet, which was accordingly appropriated to the purpose.

This boundary planting must also follow the south line, and it was so extended on the paper plan, as one of the necessary future features. Then the west side, an equal distance from the axis, was drawn in. This left a simple

rectangular plot behind the house balanced on the axis.
Built that way, the garden would have been orderly in
design but stupidly uninteresting.

In a region where all is straight lines and rectangles,
a curving shape is a relief. Consequently, a half circle
was drawn at the farther end of the axis, opening toward
the lawn. It was made larger and smaller, nearer and
farther from the end, until it looked right on paper. When
such a shape looks right on paper it is more apt than not
to look right on the ground, although sometimes it will
have to be changed when the actual work is under way.

The corners outside the central rectangle were made
larger, of course, as the rectangle was shortened to make
room for the semicircle. Where the neighborhood is particularly ugly, it would pay to use all the extra corner-
area for tall-growing trees. A tiny opening under them
could be used for a secluded bench and table. In the example it is assumed that such a screen is already provided
by the existing trees, so no such heavy corner-planting is
needed. Consequently, the corners can be used as beds
for vegetables and roses.

The semicircle, being the termination of the view along
the axis from the house, must be emphasized. The outdoor
living-room could go there, and serve the purpose effectively.
But it would then lie at an inconvenient distance from the
house. It would face the larger building. It would be pleasanter to face the west from which one could see the sunsets
that are hidden from the house-terrace by the kitchen wing.
It is thus set back in the boundary planting on the east
side of the rectangle, halfway to the back of the lot. It
would be solidly built up on the side toward the neighbor.
Here one could then see more sky and fewer buildings, or

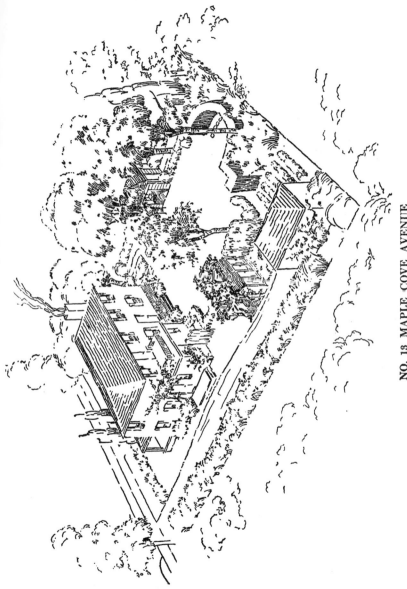

NO. 13 MAPLE COVE AVENUE

perhaps none, if the planting along the drive be clever enough.

For convenience and variety, a narrow path is carried through the boundary planting from the outdoor living-room to the rose bed in the southeast corner. This path then turns to reach the main grass panel next the semicircle.

At the end of the axis, in the semicircle, a little bird-fountain is placed to focalize attention. It is reached by a stepping-stone path. In order to get a mass of color at this important spot, the rest of the semicircle is filled with herbaceous flowers. To outline the back of it, and to screen the next lot, a high hedge is planted.

To outline the shape of the grass rectangle and edge the boundary planting, the tall hedge behind the semicircle is turned to go in front of the shrubbery, but kept down to one foot in height with larger clipped balls or cubes at the corners and beside the paths.

On the west side, a thin screen of some sort is appropriate to shut off the laundry yard, vegetable garden, and garage. It may be of posts and slats for grapes or flowering vines; an elaborate trellis pleasant to see; or merely a line of pole beans or blackberry bushes — temporarily at least. The little edging-hedge is carried down this side, too. Between it and the screen is room for a narrow bed of flowers to balance the scattered groups of perennials growing among the shrubs on the east side.

Some sort of break in the screen is needed directly opposite the outdoor living-room. It is a good place for a path through to the garage. This could be made like a short arbor separating laundry yard and vegetable garden. On it could grow grapes or even a *Forsythia suspensa*, properly trained. To make it more dark and interesting from across the lawn, the south side could be used as the back of the garden toolhouse, which would open toward the vegetable garden and cold frames.

On the west side the drive is kept close to the house to make room for a wider bed next the boundary. The space it takes would make a valuable addition to the vegetable garden. There is a serious waste here; but it is shown as an example of typical garage-location which the garden-designer must make the most of when it cannot be changed. The bed on the west boundary could be filled with trees, bushes, ferns, and so forth, which take but little attention from the gardener. Or it could change and become a rock or wild garden to be an attractive spot from the dining-room window.

On the north or street side a strip of lawn is left next the sidewalk; then a fence and tall hedge protect the house from the street. East of the house a line of fruit trees shuts out the neighboring buildings. A path lets one through to the grass-garden panel.

XIV

DETAILS OF NO. 11 MAPLE COVE AVENUE

THE garage on the preferred plan, No. 11 Maple Cove Avenue, is recessed from the street and the neighboring line far enough to be set among shrubs and trees, which would make the corner attractive in the view of the public. It is placed off the corner of the house so that all the kitchen windows get direct light and air. It is also out of the direct view from any window. The side and rear serve as walls enclosing the front yard and laundry yard. Planted with vines or covered with trellises, these walls can be good-looking and will help much to keep street nuisances at a distance. The obvious convenience to the automobile driver is indisputable.

These same arguments in favor of its corner location are equally strong for the neighbor on the west. At first sight, and more especially from the outside, a corner location appears to be in the way. But, as a matter of fact, it is the least objectionable site from the neighbor's point of view, giving him the maximum light and air in his windows and being least conspicuous from within his rooms.

Where restrictions or other conditions make such a location impossible, it can be shoved back on a line with the house. Such a scheme can be made attractive. The two buildings may, for instance, be connected by a free-standing wall with an arched gate in it. And as a garage roof is low, it need not cut off all light even from the first-story windows. In such an event, the area before set apart for the laundry yard is given to the garage, and the laundry yard has to take some of the all too little space allotted to the vegetable garden. Every foot that the garage is set back from the street must be paid for in the reduction of garden space without adequate return either in practical convenience, in economy of construction, or in sightliness.

The fence along the sidewalk is set back at No. 11 as at No. 13 — in this case to continue the street side of the garage. The planting along the fence would be the same, with a narrow lawn on the sidewalk for the public benefit. The enclosed yard-vestibule between fence and house would be rather impersonal — tidy, first of all. As it would be north of the house, it would be in the shade pretty much all the time. Garden flowers could not be successfully grown there and a lawn would be weeds and patches in no time. Evergreen Japanese yews or rhododendrons would probably succeed in pairs inside the gate and beside the porch.

A narrow bed around the area could be filled with ferns, wild wood-flowers, spring bulbs, and so on, with a few shade enduring shrubs to give body and character to the masses. In acid-soil country, *Azalea vaseyi* and *A. arborescens* would be pink in springtime, mountain laurel in June, *Azalea viscosa* (swamp honeysuckle) white and fragrant in July. A few ground hemlocks (*Taxus canadensis*) would give a touch of evergreen. In neutral or alkaline soils the azaleas and rhododendrons would succeed only when the chemical reaction of the soil had been changed. Box would do well if the climate permitted. Tree box grows fairly fast and slips borrowed from a neighbor could be easily rooted at home. Japanese yew would do well. Japanese holly, an excellent, broad-leaved evergreen similar to box, in spite of a doubtful reputation thrives in the severe climate of western New York. Evergreen thorn (*Pyracantha coccinea lalandi*) is an exceptionally beautiful small tree which is worth trying in a protected place. Several of the evergreen *euonymus* would sprawl about in the shade even if they did not get bushy. *E. radicans latifolia* and *E. carrierei* appear to do somewhat better than *E. radicans vegetus* in alkaline soil, though there is no apparent reason for this. The holly-leaved barberries (*mahonia*) are worth a trial.

Some of these plants are expensive if bought in large sizes, but fairly cheap when small. The *euonymus* is particularly easy to root from cuttings. With a frame or two the enterprising gardener can grow plants from cuttings in a surprisingly short time, that would cost hundreds of dollars if bought from nurseries. Frames are exceedingly important if one has but little money to spend.

Where grass will not thrive in shade, the ground can be covered with myrtle (*Vinca minor*), *Pachysandra terminalis* (which is so useful as to be stupidly overplanted at times), or English ivy, which will thrive on the ground in situations where it winter-kills on walls. In alkaline soils a few Christmas roses (*Helleborus niger*) will thrive, though it spreads slowly. It seems to prefer a place under trees among the tangled roots. Wintergreen (*Gaultheria procumbens*), partridge berry (*Mitchella repens*), mountain cranberry (*Vaccinium vitis-idæa*), bearberry (*Arctostaphylos uva-ursi*) are perhaps the handsomest of all groundcovers in acid-soil countries. The last two are difficult to establish, but worth an effort. The mountain cranberry seems to like upland peat with very little soil mixed in. The

NO. 11 MAPLE COVE AVENUE

bearberry prefers almost pure sand and a glaring sun, though it flourishes in fairly heavy woods at home. Money-wort (*Lysimachia nummularia*) and bugle (*Ajuga reptans*) are almost fool-proof. They are a blessed last resort.

It is not easy to explain just how to design an informal lawn or garden. A paper plan doesn't help one much. The first effort goes to intensive study of the existing area, whether large or small. Unless it is utterly devoid of any living rock or plant, it will disclose some clue to the earnest seeker. Even when covered with débris and ashes, some chance hillock, the location of a contractor's tool-box, will intimate the right or wrong place for a rock garden or shrub plantation. If there is nothing on the lot itself, then the neighborhood, good, bad, or indifferent, will suggest that it be left open to see, entirely shut out, or left open here and there where some bit of treetop and sky in the distance should not be hidden though the neighboring houses must be thickly screened. This sort of study takes time on the part of the beginning gardener. Changing conditions must be watched from hour to hour, with sun and moon, on good days and bad. Hurried planning is invariably a mistake.

All trace of original vegetation and ground formation are not apt to be entirely erased when a building is begun, though contractors' men will soon spoil it all with trucks, piles of excavated dirt and inept " grading " to a level, if given their own way. It is twice — four times as hard to design a good informal garden on a lot that has been newly graded. This grading — which is more often than not called for in the house contract — regularly destroys more beauty than it creates. It is responsible for most of the commonplaceness of small lots. It is done first, to get rid of the excavated soil, and secondly, to leave everything in a neat and clean condition. Neat and clean little areas have no inspiration for the garden designer. Better far a hole filled with thistles.

Where the original vegetation is left, it should all be regarded as valuable until the contrary is proved. Many people have curious, senseless prejudices about growing things. They respect, even love trees, though they be ugly, decrepit specimens in the wrong place. Men are apt to have the strongest feeling about trees, which they will not touch, no matter how they interfere with each other or with other things. There are weeds among trees as there are among flowers. Weedy trees, especially where they crowd and spoil better varieties, should be eradicated like any other weed. On the other hand, neither men nor women seem to have a natural regard for native plants of less than tree-stature. They waste no thought upon shrubs, except for a few rare varieties, and then only during the flowering season. Yet many shrubs are more beautiful and more appropriate to certain situations than any tree could be. The order will go forth to the Italian laborer to " clear the ground " of everything but the precious trees, which are to be jealously protected.

The wise gardener will study the shrubs, even the native plants and ground-cover, as carefully as the trees. Where desirable, trees will be cut to give the shrubs a better chance. In any case, the insensate order to " clear the ground " will never be given. Many a man has destroyed thousands of plants on his land, which, later, with more knowledge, he replaced at great cost from a nursery. A typical example is the common New England aster which grows everywhere by the roadsides and in the edges of fields and meadows. The new gardener cleans it out, then buys it from the nursery for a couple of dollars a dozen to put in his flower beds. Yet he no doubt prides himself on being a " practical, economical man with no nonsense about him."

One of the pleasures of an informal garden or lawn is the trees, which are a necessary part of its charm instead of a horticultural nuisance as they prove to be in formal flower-beds. On the small place, especially, the refreshment of shade is many hundred per cent more grateful than the brightest herbaceous border. It is pleasant to have them both, but shade comes first. Consequently, no plan is a good one which needlessly sacrifices good trees, or one which needlessly keeps poor — or even good — trees in the wrong place.

The lots for which the plans are shown (see page 84) have, each of them, five trees in the southeast corner. The formal garden at No. 13, as well as the informal lawn, is designed to keep them all, though in the former case the flower bed in the half circle, and the surrounding hedge would be something of a problem if the two trees on the south border were very large. As we are permitted to assume anything, it is supposed that they are old pear trees, — nothing is handsomer in a flower garden, — birches, shads, or straggly dogwoods.

The border planting is equally necessary in all cases. But in the informal garden the shrubs are not in a straight bed. They are irregularly scattered and spaced as will look best when reasonably well grown. They are not put in beds with wiggly outlines on the edge of the lawn. Instead, the lawn is fitted to the shrubs after the planting is done (see page 101).

Where the shade is most dense on the east side of the

lawn — in the formal plan the location of the outdoor living-room — a platform level with the ground is made where
grass will not grow. It is partly gravel, partly flat stone
or bricks left when the house was done, or from some old
place in the neighborhood recently torn up. Benches,
tables, and chairs, dull in color and comfortable to sit on,
stay on this platform all summer. During part of the
day it is cooler than any other spot out of doors, and
mosquitoes are troublesome only a small part of each
summer.

Beyond, the planting widens to fill most of the corner.
A rather wide path twists between the bushes. At the
farthest corner in the deep shade, where it is visible from
the house, a picturesque jar is set under the trees. It
will also be seen from a bench by a pool farther west.
From most places the jar will be hidden. Where it would
unbalance the composition of trees, bushes, and structures,
it must be out of sight. Restraint in the use of decoration
must be practised in all gardens.

The main axis of the garden, prolonged on the living-
room door and terrace steps, is almost disguised by un-
symmetrical planting, but it must not be forgotten on that
account. To fix attention at the terminus, a small irregular
pool is built as part of the rock-garden screen at the back.
A trickle of water comes out between two rocks higher up
into a tiny pocket of water, from which it drops two or
three different ways over the edges of the stones to the
main pool at the bottom. This pool is small, and is made
to look like a natural spring such as is often found at the
foot of large boulders. The bottom of the pool is paved
with flat stones to enhance the effect. All signs of cement
in the joints of the stones are hidden behind moss and

plants. West of the pool, well hidden by the bushes from the house, is a wood bench where one can watch the birds in the water and the bees thirstily drinking from tiny rivulets, smell the roses, and forget the book at one's side.

On looking back from the pool, the house seems rather bare. Anything in the shape of beds of planting would merely stuff the place up, detracting from the simple, open lawn-area at the house end. Anything next the steps would be crowded. Instead, specimen bushes at the corners of the terrace, equi-spaced from the axis, would be better. They must be alike save for flower color, possibly. This is an ideal place for specimen plants — sunny, protected, and alone. Nothing should be put in which will in time cover the windows of dining-room or outdoor living-room. Otherwise it is the place for the favorite plant of the gardener-designer.

The west side of the lawn is marked by a thin screen toward the rose bed and vegetable garden, which is extended from the southwest corner of the house. This screen does not need to be very high or thick. It is pleasant to get a glimpse of the other gardens beyond. But it must be a recognizable partition, following the rule of the separation of garden units.

The ground next this screen on the lawn side would get the morning sun. Many herbaceous and other plants should do well there. A herbaceous border would not be objectionable. But the outline toward the lawn should not be a straight line, which would be out of harmony with the informal shapes of the planting elsewhere. The plants would soon push out toward the grass. Let them indicate the outline of the bed.

In order that the bright color of this border should not

overbalance the picture as seen from the terrace, it should be planted with masses of green to separate the flowers, instead of an over-all bloom. This is the easier way to plant a bed, as a matter of fact, as one need only keep flowers of the same season together. Then clumps of flowering plants which will be suited to the places should be planted here and there among the shrubs on the east and south sides of the garden. Foxgloves, cimicifuga, some lilies, funkias, and so on, would grow happily enough in such positions.

In the southwest open corner is a little garden which may be devoted to any purpose. It is convenient, yet apart, and hence a good place for roses which are shabby during much of the year. It is a small area and may be enclosed at little expense with its own special decorative lattice, which should be covered with climbing roses. It would be separated from the vegetable and cut-flower garden by the long shallow toolhouse which would open on the north side.

The west border of the vegetable garden would probably be of blackberries or some other useful fruit that makes a good barrier. Near the toolhouse would be the frames for propagating. The path down the garden would run along the east side, which would be shaded from the morning sun by the screen next the lawn. Otherwise, the place would be left as one big bed, as is most easily managed for lines of vegetables and cut flowers. The support for the clotheslines would make a lattice separating it on the north from the laundry yard.

In the northeast corner lies a strip of land that is separated from the garden by the outdoor living-room and from the street by the fence and planting. It is not very large, but plenty wide enough for a central path with a boundary planting on the east and a bed next the house. While the next house would probably cut off the morning sun, yet it would get light and air. It would make an excellent special garden for iris, spring bulbs, or other plants which would make a good showing at least once during the season and be neat and unobtrusive at other times.

XV

DETAILS OF NO. 15 MAPLE COVE AVENUE

A WASTEFUL PLAN

It would be a waste of time to consider a ground plan with no points to recommend it. It is, however, worth while to discover what is wrong with a scheme that is the result of misdirected work. The plan for No. 15 Maple Cove Avenue is typical of a large number of well-intentioned small places in this country. They show a real desire to do the right thing. But they fail for two reasons. First, they try to follow little-understood and often false prejudices of current garden-design which themselves are but modernized versions of the senseless habits of gardeners of the Victorian carpet-bedding period. Secondly, they lack any real sense of the necessary organization of the garden- and landscape-plan.

Plan-organization, as was indicated in Chapter V, means the right relationship of all features of a place to each other, both great and small. The good plan considers the whole lot as the unit into which each detail must fit as may be best — not only for itself but for every other detail on the place. There should not be one square foot of waste area on a lot any more than there would be in a house that is well planned. In the middle of the last century American houses were built with dark chasms under front stairs; with long, wasteful Stygian corridors and halls between every two rooms, almost; with big apartments and no comfort anywhere.

That sort of thing has gone for ever. Nowadays the least experienced home-builder is able to argue with his architect about the intensive use of every square foot under the roof. House plans that make the most of all the area are the rule, not the exception.

Equal care directed to economical use of the outdoor areas will be the next move of home-builders. In order to do away with waste out of doors, they will have to study the organization of the plan, just as they did in working over the house plan.

As a useful exercise, let us measure the wasted areas or those that might be put to better use on the plan of 15 Maple Cove Avenue (page 84). The whole front yard is presented to the public, adding apparently to the width of the street, of which it makes a parkway. There are miles of these little parkways in every American town and city. They are pretty, to be sure. But they altogether lack the charm of the old New England village street with its fences along the sidewalk and its front yards full of flowers that are largely hidden behind old lilacs and snowballs. Any sacrifice of home privacy and comfort due to throwing open all the land to public view is wasteful. What is more, it defeats its own purpose. For, in the last analysis, the beauty of a street of residences lies in one's conviction that the places are true homes of true Americans, living a quiet, comfortable family life in all self-respect. Privacy is an essential quality of family life, and privacy cannot exist, out of doors, where the public can see front, sides, and even the back of detached houses. At best one feels that the real life of the inhabitant is driven indoors. And it is the purpose of gardeners to let it out to light, sunshine, and flowers.

The plan indicates that the house is heavily belted with base- or foundation-planting. This treatment has become a rule of thumb for the unthinking. Like all rules of thumb, it is convenient because it tells one definitely what to do when one is uncertain. Consequently, it has been largely adopted and exploited by nurserymen.

It came about in a natural way. The profession of landscape architecture began in this country in the middle of the nineteenth century when the mansard-roof house was at its worst. Those buildings were perched up on high foundations, like square, uncompromising, very ugly boxes. It was the duty of the landscape architect to take the curse off them, and the best thing he could do under the circumstances was to hide the ugly foundations and break up the harsh geometrical solids with the rounded forms of shrubs and vegetation. The fact that base-planting was first of all a necessary screen was soon forgotten. Principles of æsthetics are more interesting to professors. The secondary idea of modulation between houses and ground by means of base-planting was soon accepted as advisable in the case of all structures, even when they were beautiful to look upon. For, as time went on, the ugly box-house disappeared. After a short reaction to the other extreme, in which turrets and gingerbread work were let loose on the land, architecture began to improve. To-day many of our houses are among the most beautiful of the products of modern art. And this is as true of small as of large places. They fit snugly into the land. They have fine proportions and masses. There is no ugliness to hide. They are still geometrical forms, as all structures must be. But what is the earth to rest on, with its planes, terraces, hillocks, and swales, but geometrical form? Where is the sense of so-called modulation by means of the softness and rounded irregularity of bushes, from one geometrical form to another? The argument for modulation is gone. Instead of tying house and grounds together, foundation-planting all too often sets the house apart on a weak cushion of bushes. If the building is carefully designed to fit its place, the lines and masses can easily be spoiled by hiding them under planting. A good house can always be made more beautiful by a careful decoration of planting. But it must be sparingly used and carefully located. Base-planting around a good house, rule-of-thumb fashion, will often enough spoil the picture rather than help it.

On the other hand, not all modern houses are beautiful. Many of them are still strangely ugly in spite of the good models. Ugly fountains are still being built. In such cases, the old rules hold — where there is an unsightly thing, hide it behind bushes and vines. Hide nothing that is beautiful.

Thus, for reasons of both privacy and appearance, it would be well to take the planting away from the house foundation of No. 15 (see page 84) and make a hedge of it along the sidewalk, leaving only a couple of shapely bushes on either side of the steps and here and there elsewhere if the appearance of the house will be improved by them.

West of the house the entire area — except for a hedge along the line — is given over to garage and drive. The wastefulness of this disposition of the land has been already dwelt upon.

East of the house, between it and the neighbor's place, is an artistic vacuum, such as exists up and down all our streets. It fulfills no purpose. It is neither useful nor beautiful. It is planted with grass because the owner gave it no thought. It is waste land.

South of the house is the only considerable area to be given over to gardening. There is a real difference of feeling about the desirability of having a flower garden next to the house. Either one likes it or one doesn't like it. In any case it is evident that only the fanatical gardener is satisfied to look from his windows all winter long upon the emptiness of muddy flower-beds. It is wiser to have a bit of grass next the house, even if it is but the central panel of a flower garden which thus combines garden and lawn, as at No. 13. In any event, this lawn must be purposeful. To be agreeable to look on, it must have shape and background. It must not slide off into another bit of lawn with which it is not reasonably connected — as with the east strip in this case and the area between kitchen and laundry yard.

If a garden is to occupy part of the south area, it should be definitely fitted into place. Here — as so often elsewhere — it seems to have been dropped down in the middle of the lawn, the breadth of which it thus destroys. It could be much improved without marked change by filling with a shrub-border east of the flower garden and west to the laundry yard, making a second definitely enclosed lawn at the farther end of the place. This enclosure would go all round it, cutting off the vegetable bed. The frank partition of areas must never be forgotten.

This formal garden is a silly pattern for such an area. It has a strongly marked axis and cross-axis of its own. But these fundamental characteristics of its plan have no reference to anything else on the place. They begin nowhere and they lead nowhere. A scheme of the same sort which was laid out with reference to one of the living-room windows, or perhaps with a path opposite the rear hall door, would have had something at least to tie it to the house and so put it in definite relation with other and more important elements of the place. The cross-axis could have been made a continuation of the walk to the garage south of the laundry yard, if nothing more. As it is, neither the extreme length nor the width of the area have been taken advantage of.

In order to do this, there is no need of keeping the whole place open from one end to the other. Assuming that a complicated system of paths and beds like this flower garden were desirable in approximately the same place, a mere glimpse from house window or door clean through the garden to some object at the south side of the property would have served to make the place seem much deeper and more interesting. In the plan, every such chance is wasted.

Obviously, no survey of all the existing conditions was made before the plan was begun. And — equally obviously — no two of the features were laid out with any reference to each other. The place has no organization. It is, of necessity, wasteful and dull.

XVI

THE TRAVELER SEES THE LITTLE GARDEN

GARDENS have claimed the attention of observant travelers as far back as traveling is recorded. Indeed, our liveliest and probably truest ideas of long-scattered civilizations are aroused by the relics of garden-descriptions which we have inherited. The appeal of gardens to simple minds is no less potent than to the sophisticated. If words have souls, as some have claimed, then we must believe that the soul of the word " garden " is revealed to man first and perhaps most intensely of all objects outside himself and his kind. The word " home " appears in but few languages. It would be interesting to know if the " home " as meaning primarily the habitation did not belong exclusively to peoples who live where long cold winters have kept them much indoors — where safety and comfort are identified with roof, walls, and fire, rather than the vine, the rose, and the fountain, the symbols of civilization in more clement latitudes.

In any event, we know that the love of home has always been one of our deepest human feelings. And Southern peoples who lack the term " home " do not need it, I believe, because they have the word " garden " to take its place. Such a conjecture seems reasonable, at least to a lover of gardens. The Garden of Eden is known by all who have heard of the Bible; the Hanging Gardens of Babylon alone are popularly remembered of all the ancient Wonders of the World; a mere phrase, "Persian gardens," is enough to justify a forgotten civilization. One of the vast palaces of the world moulders away at Granada, neglected beside the famous gardens of the Alhambra. Certainly gardens mean more than palaces in the happy souvenirs of men. Unfortunately, the grandiose has always attracted observers almost to the exclusion of modest gardens, so that we are without information about the past that would be useful in studying our own little problems.

There is much to be learned in foreign lands from those who have had the piling centuries to experiment in. The little gardens of the world are very different from each other, just as the nations differ. But they have their similarities, too, which are based on experience of common needs. The designer of a little garden in America will do well to observe some of the types evolved by his ancestors and the ancestors of his fellow countrymen.

The small garden in Italy is the most simple and frank. With all its ancient pomp and heraldry, there is a democracy in the domestic affairs of Italy that is hard for the modern American to understand. With few exceptions the country home of the grandee was and still is both mansion and farmhouse. Grain is stored over the drawing-room. The Duke oversees the harvest. His lady marries off, with a high hand, Giovanni the stable boy and Lucia the beaming village beauty. The contacts everywhere are decidedly intimate, to the point where servants, while passing the salad, give their opinions without the faintest trace of impertinence.

In certain great houses the customs may have changed in imitation of the English models. But, in general, master and man are thrown more closely together than is the case here.

In much the same way the various functions of the household are less strictly separated than with us. Some of the rooms and even in some cases part of the gardens are made private apartments and thus reserved for the owner. But most of the place, both indoors and out, is free to all, and the smaller proprietors, at least, have no objection to spending many of their waking hours, when not actually in company with their people, in the courtyards and gardens that are used in common.

The Italian climate invites one to spend much of the time out of doors all the year round, which has had a definite effect on the design of houses and gardens. Indeed, many rooms of the farm-villas are little more than loggias or open sheds, with protection against sun and rain but otherwise not enclosed. Attached to the buildings are supports for the grape, generally of barked poles, sometimes supported on stone columns, much like an old-fashioned American grape arbor with a flat vine-covered roof. This makes a pleasant shady place for much of the humble work of the establishment during the day and a bit of repose or play almost any time, but more especially in the cool of the evening.

In the course of time these little gardens — for such they are — become furnished with useful things. Benches are built into the walls between the poles. Big oil-jars are conveniently left about. A fountain of running water is introduced from some spring or stream. Strings of peppers are hung up under the eaves to dry. Pots on a parapet are filled with vegetables and flowers mixed up together. At one side is a fig tree, at another an oleander. The ground is rarely level and is stepped in irregular terraces which closely follow the original topography, either up or down from the building. Steps mount and descend at convenient intervals to reach the lines of grapes, olives, lemons, or oranges. Here and there a cypress — to the perennial astonishment of admiring New Englanders — pushes up to jostle the clouds overhead. If there is room, a low spreading live oak enfolds a dark tunnel running away from the gate beyond a flat terrace lying in the pale green shadow of clipped plane-trees. The ground is bare. One does not miss green grass.

Nothing could be more simple or more frank. Work and play both have their place. Use and ornament combine, then separate again, both present everywhere. They were conceived together in every detail, more often unconsciously than consciously. Probably the uneducated Italian does not stop to realize that they are separate functions of material things, until he reaches this country where they are too often shamelessly divorced. Even so, an efficiency expert could learn much from the extraordinarily practical and intensive way in which the land is employed and cultivated. Its use is beautiful. Its beauty is used. Is that the cause of the perfume of romance that hangs over it all?

The little garden in Italy is much the same, whether about the peasant's house or the villa of the gentleman farmer. Use and comfort combined with ornament, following the lines of the buildings, street, and the changes of topography without thought for formal or informal design, has left them very picturesque. But the almost public use of the small farmyard-garden precludes any real sense of privacy in the American sense, though the highways be shut off with high walls and gates.

The Frenchman is more sophisticated and far more taken up with the forms and conventions of life. The smallest landed proprietor is proud of his place in the petite bourgeoisie, feeling vastly superior to the domestics of his household, who, in turn, look up to the patron. On the small farms, perhaps, conditions resemble those of Italy. But the little gardens that crowd into memory belong rather to the towns and small cities.

There the gardens no longer run into the houses through loggias and sheds. The house is a unit by itself. The garden is a thing apart. At the same time, the two seem to grow out of each other and neither can be properly studied alone. The Frenchman, more than any other member of the families of western civilization save possibly the Spaniard, lives a family life of extreme seclusion. Group intimacies are rare among neighbors. Running in and out is not encouraged. Entertainment always has a touch of formality, even in the simplest homes. The heart of the family is not exposed for daws to peck at. Even within the household, the gulf is constantly felt between members of the family and the domestics, although contacts are so intimate as to bewilder an American who has not breathed in the caste system from his first moment. All these characteristics and many more are revealed in their gardens and the life lived therein.

At one side or at the back of the house the low windows of drawing-room or dining-room give on to a balcony or narrow terrace that leads down into the garden. It is apt to be small — even microscopic as gardens go. Even city palace-gardens are rarely larger than a good-sized suburban lot. They are invariably enclosed with high walls, which give all the seclusion of an interior room. Even the smallest seem to have room for a tree whose deep shade cools most of the garden and house. Yet there is always a sunny corner, too, for chilly days where a chair and the inevitable iron table can be withdrawn from the sharp air-currents. A path sometimes makes a straight way but more often meanders to the iron gate which holds off the outer world. It is a wide path, much wider than one would find here in a small garden. In the constant shade of the tree, or at some strategic point near the house terrace, it broadens out as a platform of gravel, where one sits. There is a plot of grass to repose the eye, that may be walked upon if it is old and firm. But it does not exist for that purpose, which is better served by the path. Nor is grass an ubiquitous ground-cover. It is used only where a green carpet is wanted, as with a textile indoors. The Frenchman will tell you that a variety of materials, properly assembled, gives more interest than can possibly be derived from the exclusive use of any one. So grass is limited to what become decorative panels and is kept away from heavy shade where it never does well. Graveled areas and the brown earth are equally beautiful to his discriminating eyes. And beds of violets, English ivy, and ferns are more to his fancy than failing spotted grass-turf. One returns to the old word " elegance " in describing French gardens.

Where he has the sun, a grapevine grows over his door and a great rosebush fills the quiet place with perfume and color. Old shrubs soften the corners. Moss gathers under the ivy on the walls. Somewhere he sees the gray-blue sky. The parish church near by has a chime of bells.

Here it is that the French family live as quiet and remote as within the house. It is a calm resort for monsieur to read the Paris paper and retail the news while madame

sews or shells the early peas. On the grass the servant
puts the fine linen to bleach in safety. The children amuse
themselves, but never seem to romp into the choice begonias
like their American contemporaries. Everywhere is per-
sonified the immemorial order of French family life.

Plants, shrubs, and trees are more important in the
little garden of France than in Italy where they are almost supererogatory. This is because — for one thing —
the climate is propitious for vegetation, and many more
varieties can be grown without excessive care. But here,
too, one feels that they are but material chosen for decoration and protection, which might have been otherwise provided with almost as much satisfaction. The vegetable
kingdom seems to be regarded much as by the painter for
its decorative worth, or by the truck gardener for its eco-
nomic value. Of course, many a Frenchman loves growing
things for themselves. But not with the passion of more
Northern folk.

Yet his little garden is one of the characteristic charms
of this intensely domestic creature, a part of his daily life
as dear to him as his house, apart from which he could not
think of home.

In England we find the garden of our own tradition. The
first moment an American steps into a small English garden remains a tender memory always. It seems unap-
proachably comfortable to his restless searching eyes. It
is leisure, at last, for his spirit.

Without doubt his introduction through the lazy rich
countryside helps the impression. English country seems
so fit a setting for kindly, tranquil homes that the traveler
is ready with all generous adjectives before the gate is un-
latched. And the delight of the place far exceeds his own

imagining. The reason is, I believe, that the countryside disclosed to him, who was accustomed to less regulated — if not actually savage — American scenery, a revelation of the beauty of order in nature. For, with all her obvious service to man, English country seems first of all to be natural.

The little English garden has this expected order and more. It has the order of art in control of nature. This is perhaps the apotheosis of man's objective effort, the greatest contribution that England has made to the fine arts. Of course, not all English gardens, especially grandiose English gardens, are beautiful. But the old small home-gardens are all that one dreams a garden should be.

Their relation to the house is unlike that of the small Italian or French garden. In the first they seemed to be part one of the other. In the second they were cleverly united and on a par. In the last the garden — or rather, one should say the grounds, to be better understood, perhaps — seems to be the major unit of which the house is but one, though that the most conspicuous, element. Even so, they were obviously designed together to benefit each other. Each one without the other would be incomplete.

Here, as elsewhere in Europe, withdrawal from the outer world — seclusion — is the first and most important of garden qualities. Walls or hedges surround the whole place, ensuring reposeful privacy, without which no garden can be fully used and enjoyed. The Englishman's home is his castle, and he wisely includes his garden as part of his home. Even within his walls he wants privacy. To get it he has organized the business of his household so that the service and residence quarters are well separated. The garden is for the recreation of family and guests alone.

And it is made to care for many. For he is warmly hospitable to his friends.

Except for the cottage gardens, which are jolly little places immensely interesting to the gardener who specializes in horticulture, the English home gardens are somewhat larger, on the average, than the European. They cover from one to four acres. In America they would seem to be fairly large, as here the whole estate would be no larger. And it is in this point that the difference can be explained. In America the garden, like the house, is a thing by itself, separate from the lawns and service quarters, both in position and design. In England the whole place is one garden, designed as a landscape unit which includes house, garage, and service quarters as well as lawn and garden. The results go to prove that this is the right way to solve the problem. The English lawns are gardens. They are enclosed areas, arranged and planted for convenience, comfort, and beauty.

While in principle they differ but little from other good gardens, yet they are unique in showing a profound and affectionate understanding of plants, shrubs, and trees. During many centuries Englishmen of all classes have studied and experimented with vegetation. They now know what will thrive under varying conditions and how to maintain in the best condition what is planted. The handling of all plant material is bold and sure. The success is due in no small measure to the fact that the men are no less disciples of gardening than the women, and the boys and girls are unconsciously trained to carry on the work from generation to generation. Englishmen are the greatest sportsmen of the world, as individuals. Tiger-hunter, warrior, and statesman return home to add a new rose-bed and discuss cutworms, in happy anticipation of a future time when all their days can be devoted to gardening.

So it is that one finds in the Little English Garden — helped as it is not only by intelligent design and maintenance, but also by a remarkably favorable climate — perfect green lawns, luxuriant foliage-masses, fine specimen plants and a wealth of flowers. But behind it all is the mind that decrees that all these things are but added to the garden, which in itself must be — in proportion and detail — private, comfortable in all seasons, and well fitted to the use of its owner.

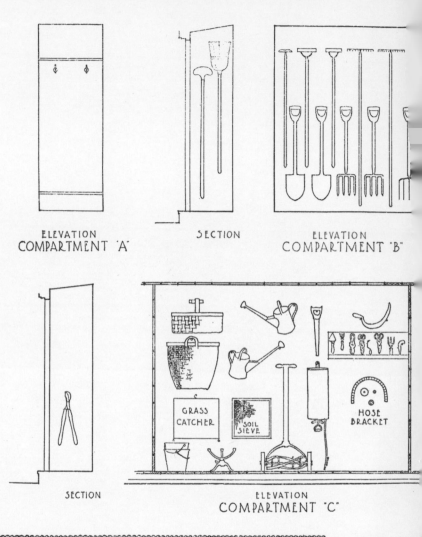

ELEVATION
COMPARTMENT "A"

SECTION

ELEVATION
COMPARTMENT "B"

SECTION

GRASS
CATCHER

SOIL
SIEVE

HOSE
BRACKET

ELEVATION
COMPARTMENT "C"

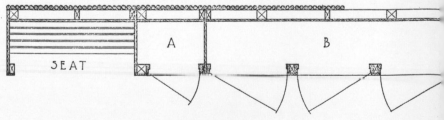

SEAT   A   B

DETAILS FOR A SMALL TOOL HOUSE
Scale ¾"=1'